The People's Rosary

Anielle Reid

THE PEOPLE'S ROSARY

Contents

Dedication	x
Preface	xi

1	Walk with Mary Through Life's Mysteries	1
2	How to Use This Book in Daily Life	4
3	The Rosary - A Timeless Prayer	5
4	How to Pray the Rosary	11
5	The Mysteries of the Rosary	16
6	Understanding the Rosary's Prayers	18
7	Understanding the Traditional Mysteries	33
8	How to Pray Through Modern Mysteries	59
9	Rosaries for Modern Day Issues	61

Living in Fear of Political Oppression	63
Peace Amid War, Genocide, and Violence	67
Wisdom in the Age of AI and Tech Overload	71
Internalized Racism and Division	75
Climate Justice and Stewardship of Creation	79
Freedom from Debt	83
Struggling with Immigration and Refugee Journeys	87

10	Rosaries for Overcoming Addictions and Behaviors	92

Pornography Addiction	94
Drug Addiction	98
Disordered Eating	102
TV Addiction	106
Jealousy	110
Gossip	114
Social Media Addiction	118
Releasing Control	122
Low Self Esteem	126
11 Rosaries for Work, Career and Calling	130
Career Discernment and Clarity	132
Transitioning to a New Field or Industry	136
Job Dissatisfaction	140
Burnout and Overwhelm	144
Financial Provision Through Work	148
Discovering Your Vocation or Purpose	152
New Job or Opportunity	156
Entrepreneurial Courage and Wisdom	160
Balancing Work and Family	164
Students and Vocational Training	168
Workplace Justice and Ethical Leadership	172
12 Rosaries for Parents	177
Devotion to Our Lady of La Leche	179
Breastfeeding	185
Post Partum	189
The Loss of a Child	194
Fertility and Family Planning	200

Protecting a Child from Danger	204
13 Rosaries for Family Issues	209
Patience and Understanding	211
Ancestral Healing	215
Healing Sibling Rivalry	219
Black Sheep of the Family	224
Conflict Resolution	229
Strained Relationships with Narcissistic Parents	233
Healing from Sexual Abuse within the Family	238
14 Rosaries for Romance	242
Healing After Separation or Divorce	243
Becoming a Better Romantic Partner	247
Long-Distance or Military Couples	252
Healing After a Breakup	256
Abusive Relationships	262
Healing After Betrayal or Distance	268
Shared Purpose and Mission in Love	272
Engaged and Newlywed Couples	276
Being Violated on a Date	280
Discernment in Dating	285
Sacred Union	289
Trust in Love	293
15 Rosaries for Spiritual Growth and Inner Peace	297
Peace in Anxiety	298
Brokenhearted	302
Healing Anger	306
Patience and Trust in Divine Timing	310

Fighting Obtrusive Thoughts	314
Embracing Your Spiritual Role	318
Discernment and Choosing the Light	322
Beginning New Chapters	326
Fasting and Physical Discipline	330
Connect to the Angels	334
Appendix: FAQs About the Rosary	339
About the Author	357

Copyright © 2025 by Danielle Reid

All rights reserved. No part of this book may be reproduced in any manner whatsoever without written permission except in the case of brief quotations embodied in critical articles and reviews.

First Printing, 2025

To the Blessed Virgin Mary, thank you for your presence, guidance, and protection, and for your countless manifestations.

To the angels who surround and assist Mary's children.

To my son, who inspires new prayers, my husband, an answered prayer, and my friends who share their prayers with me.

To those touched by my work—your faith and stories remind me I am seen, called, and connected.

To fellow Marians who show me I am not alone.

To the mystics who reveal Mary's truth with courage and love.

This book is both a thank you to Mary and an offering to her, as well as to all who find themselves under her mantle.

Thank you for reminding me who I am and showing me who I can become.

Preface

This book was born from a deeply personal journey and my desire to make the rosary more modern and accessible to today's world. For many, the rosary can feel confusing or out of reach, and I wanted to change that. My goal was to provide clarity on the mysteries of the rosary, presenting them in a way that resonates with people from all walks of life-whether you're a mystic, Catholic, Pentecostal, or simply someone searching for a deeper connection to Mary.

Through this book, I've re-imagined the rosary prayers to address modern-day issues and challenges, offering reflections that feel relatable and impactful. These prayers and mysteries were written with the hope of helping people overcome struggles in various parts of their lives-whether it's addiction, challenges in romance, career uncertainty, spiritual growth, or familial hardships. I also wanted to include prayers that directly address pressing concerns of our time, such as the rise of AI, political divisions, and financial instability, making these reflections even more relevant to the world we live in today.

It's my prayer that these new prayers help people feel closer to Mary and see the Bible stories in a fresh and meaningful way. Mary's love is universal, and the rosary can be too. My hope is that this book creates a bridge for anyone who wants to connect with Mary, making it easier to pray the rosary and experience its blessings in a way that feels personal, modern, and transformative.

1

Walk with Mary Through Life's Mysteries

Welcome to a journey unlike any other -a journey into the heart of Mary, the Mystical Rose, the Ark of the New Covenant and the Mother of All. This book is an invitation to walk with her, to sit in her presence, and to discover the transformative power of the Rosary as a sacred tool for connection, reflection, transformation and grace.

For centuries, Mary has been a figure of profound love, compassion, and strength. For some she is more than a mother; she is a guide, a protector, and a source of divine wisdom. Across cultures and spiritual traditions, she is revered not only as the Mother of Christ but also as a universal symbol of the sacred feminine. Whether you know her as Our Lady of Perpetual Help, Our Lady of La Leche, Theotokos, The Goddess of the West or simply as Mary, she stands ready to meet you where you are-no matter your faith, background, or beliefs.

This is not a book urging you to adopt a specific religion or doctrine. Instead, it is a book about relationship. It is about opening your heart to Mary's presence and allowing her to walk with you through the mysteries of your life. It is about discovering the Rosary as a meditative and transformative practice, one that brings clarity, healing, and miracles into your everyday experience.

The Rosary is more than a prayer; it is a bridge between the seen and unseen, the earthly and the divine. It is a gentle lasso that pulls you up into the higher realms within yourself. It is a rhythm of words and silence, a sacred dance of reflection and surrender. Through its mysteries, we are invited to reflect on the joys, sorrows, and triumphs of life-not as distant stories, but as living truths that echo in our own journeys. Each bead is a step closer to Mary, and through her, to the divine wisdom and love that she embodies.

This book is for you if you long for a deeper connection with Mary. It is for the mystics, the seekers, the spiritual wanderers who see Mary not just as a historical figure, but as a living presence. It is for those who approach her as the Divine Feminine, a source of nurturing love and sacred power. It is for those who wish to use the Rosary as a tool of evocation, for meditation, transformation and devotion to Mary.

Within these pages, you will find new mysteries unveiled-modern reflections that make the Rosary more relatable to the challenges and joys of today. You will learn about the many faces of Mary, from Our Lady of Migrants to Queen of Angels, and how her presence can bring grace and guidance to every aspect of your life. You will discover prayers and meditations that invite you to walk with her, to trust her, and to let her lead you into a deeper relationship with the divine.

Above all, this book is an invitation to experience Mary as a companion on your journey. Whether you are a mother seeking strength, a seeker longing for connection, or simply someone curious about the Rosary, Mary welcomes you with open arms. She is here to walk with you through life's mysteries, to bring light to your darkest moments, and to remind you that you are never alone. So, take a deep breath. Hold the Rosary in your hands. Let its rhythm guide you into stillness, and let Mary's presence fill your heart. This is your time to walk with her, to reflect, to pray, and to receive the graces she so lovingly offers. Together, let us begin this sacred journey.

2

How to Use This Book in Daily Life

This book is designed to be a companion for your daily spiritual practice, offering insights and prayers to guide you through life's many moments. Whether you are seeking solace, searching for answers, or simply longing to deepen your connection with Mary, you can turn to this book as a source of comfort and inspiration.

Flip to the prayers that resonate with your current circumstances or address the petitions on your heart. Are you experiencing challenges, joys, or uncertainties? Explore the prayers that align with your needs, and allow their words to uplift and center you.

If you are looking to just deepen your rosary practice, read the meditations and questions associated with the traditional mysteries-the Joyful, Sorrowful, Glorious, and Luminous Mysteries.

Ultimately, this book is meant to grow with you, adapting to your needs as you progress on your spiritual path. Lean on it daily, whether for structured prayer, spontaneous inspiration, or moments of quiet reflection, and feel Mary's loving presence guiding you through life's mysteries.

3

The Rosary - A Timeless Prayer

The Rosary is more than a prayer; it is a sacred thread that weaves together centuries of devotion, spiritual evolution, and divine grace. It is a timeless practice that has guided countless souls through life's mysteries, offering peace, clarity, and connection to the divine. Rooted in ancient traditions and enriched by Mary's ongoing presence in the world, the Rosary remains as relevant today as it was centuries ago.

THE HISTORY AND ORIGINS OF THE ROSARY

The Rosary, as we know it today, is the result of centuries of spiritual development. Its name comes from the Latin word rosarium, meaning "rose garden" or "garland of roses," symbolizing a spiritual bouquet offered to the Virgin Mary. According to tradition, Blessed Alan de la Roche had visions in which each Hail Mary recited during the Rosary transformed into a beautiful rose, creating a heavenly crown offered to the Virgin Mary. Each prayer is thus seen as a rose of devotion, a fragrant offering of love and reverence.

The use of beads for prayer predates Christianity, with ancient cultures like Hinduism and Buddhism using them for meditation and repetitive prayers. Early Christians adopted similar practices, using pebbles, knots, or cords to count prayers, especially for those unable to read or memorize the 150 Psalms. Over time, this practice evolved into what became known as the Marian Psalter, a precursor to the modern rosary, allowing the faithful to meditate on the life of Christ and deepen their connection with God.

The formal development of the Rosary is often attributed to St. Dominic in the 13th century. According to tradition, during a time of great spiritual crisis for Catholics, when the Cathars were in conflict with the Church, the Virgin Mary appeared to St. Dominic and entrusted him with the Rosary as a spiritual weapon to inspire faith and combat perceived heretical teachings. While historical evidence suggests the Rosary evolved gradually, St. Dominic's role in promoting it as a tool for evangelization and devotion laid the foundation for its widespread use.

Over the centuries, the Rosary continued to evolve. By the 15th century, the modern form of the Hail Mary was established, and the Rosary took on its familiar structure of five decades, each containing ten Hail Marys and one Our Father. The addition of mysteries—Joyful, Sorrowful, Glorious, and later the Luminous Mysteries introduced by Pope St. John Paul II in 2002—invites the faithful to reflect on pivotal events in the lives of Jesus and Mary. This evolution demonstrates the Rosary's enduring ability to adapt and remain meaningful across generations.

WHY THE ROSARY REMAINS RELEVANT TODAY

The Rosary remains profoundly relevant today because Mary is still with us, still calling us to pray her Rosary. Throughout history, she has appeared to guide, comfort, and urge humanity toward prayer, repentance, and trust in God's grace. Her apparition in Kibeho, Africa, as "Our Lady of Sorrows," is a powerful reminder—she asked for prayer and repentance in the face of looming violence, offering hope to a nation on the edge of tragedy. Just as she intervened then, she continues to ask us to turn to the Rosary, not only to avoid calamities but to receive the graces she desires to pour out on her children.

The Rosary provides exactly what the world needs today. In a society grappling with chaos, moral decay, and spiritual sickness, people are crying out for healing, guidance, and peace. Mary, as our loving mother, hears this cry and calls us closer through the Rosary. Its graces are as essential now as ever, offering strength to conquer personal struggles and battles with sin. As the world turns increasingly toward spirituality to cope with uncertainty and despair, the Rosary stands as a lifeline to divine love and protection.

The world is yearning for its mother—a presence that offers comfort, hope, and healing in the face of a seemingly crumbling society. Through the Rosary, Mary invites us to let her guide us away from darkness and into the light of God's love. Her call is as urgent and relevant today as it ever was, and the Rosary remains a timeless prayer for a world in desperate need of grace.

THE SPIRITUAL BENEFITS OF PRAYING THE ROSARY

The Rosary is a prayer of transformation. It invites us to meditate on Scripture and the divine mysteries highlighted within it, drawing us closer to the divine. Each bead is a step on a sacred journey, a moment of reflection that deepens our understanding.

A Path to Peace and Clarity

The Rosary's meditative nature helps quiet the mind and focus the heart. In a world filled with distractions, it offers a sanctuary of stillness where we can encounter God's presence. Saint John Paul II described the Rosary as "a prayer of great significance, destined to bring forth a harvest of holiness." By meditating on its mysteries, we find peace amidst life's challenges and clarity in times of confusion.

A Connection to Mary's Maternal Care

Through the Rosary, we invite Mary into our lives as a loving mother and guide. Her intercession brings comfort, protection, and grace. Many have experienced miracles and answered prayers through their devotion to the Rosary, trusting in Mary's promise: "You shall obtain all you ask of me by the recitation of the Rosary."

A Deeper Mystical Understanding

For some, the Rosary opens the door to a profound, mystical understanding of Mary and the Bible. Mystics like Neville Goddard saw Mary not only as the mother of Christ but as a symbol of divine imagination and spiritual awakening within us. Praying the Rosary can inspire a deeper connection to the mysteries of the Bible, helping you see it as a psychological and mystical text that speaks to the unfolding of spiritual truths in our own lives.

A Weapon for Spiritual Healing

The Rosary has long been recognized as a powerful tool for spiritual warfare and healing. It has been used in exorcisms, as a shield against evil, and as a source of strength for those battling addictions or personal struggles. As Saint Padre Pio famously said, "The Rosary is the weapon for these times." Throughout history, men have prayed the Rosary before going into battle, seeking divine intervention to win the spiritual fight before engaging in the physical one. This was profoundly evident in the famous Battle of Lepanto in 1571, where the Christian fleet, united in prayer through the Rosary, triumphed against the Ottomans, preserving Europe's Christian heritage. The Rosary continues to be a weapon of faith, fortifying individuals in their spiritual battles today.

A Communal Prayer of Unity

The Rosary unites people in prayer, fostering a sense of community and shared faith. Whether prayed in families, parishes, confraternities, or global gatherings, it strengthens spiritual bonds and promotes unity. Within confraternities, members join together in a powerful collective devotion, amplifying its spiritual impact.

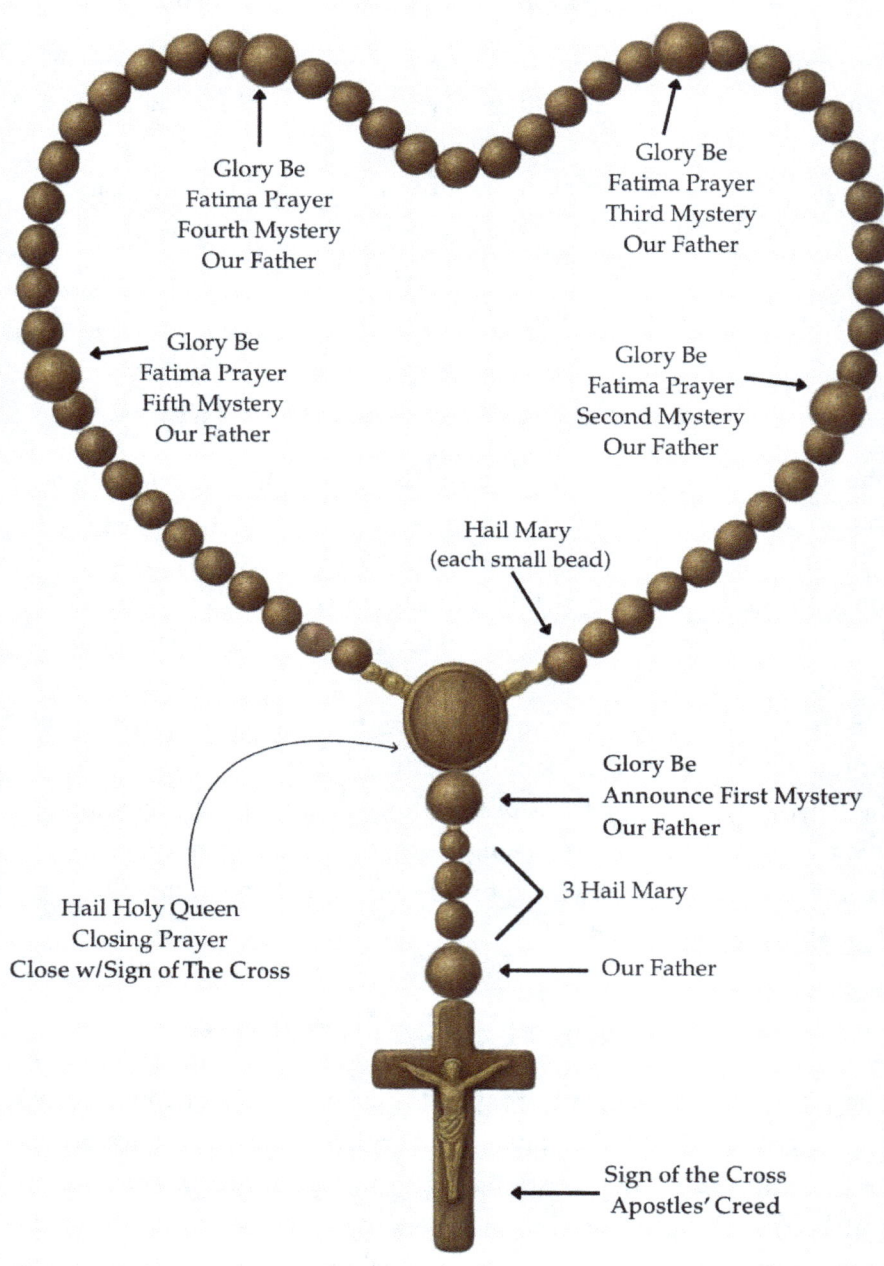

4

How to Pray the Rosary

The Rosary is a sacred and transformative prayer, a spiritual journey that invites you to walk hand in hand with Mary through the mysteries of life. While its structure is simple, its depth is profound, offering a meditative rhythm that connects the heart, mind, and soul to the divine. Though there are many kinds of rosaries and chaplets dedicated to specific devotions, this chapter will focus on the traditional Marian Rosary. Whether you are new to the Rosary or seeking to deepen your practice, this chapter will guide you through its steps, prayers, and mysteries, helping you make it a meaningful part of your spiritual life.

The Structure of the Rosary

The Rosary is composed of a sequence of prayers and meditations, guided by a string of beads. Each bead represents a prayer, and the arrangement of the beads helps you move through the decades and mysteries with ease. The Rosary is traditionally divided into five decades, each focusing on a specific mystery from the life of Jesus and Mary. The basic structure includes:

1. The Cross: Begin with the crucifix, where you make the Sign of the Cross and recite the Apostles' Creed.

2. The Pendant Beads: These include one large bead and three smaller beads. The large bead is for the Our Father, and the three smaller beads are for Hail Marys, traditionally offered for faith, hope, and charity.

3. The Decades: Each decade consists of one large bead (Our Father) and ten smaller beads (Hail Marys), followed by a Glory Be.

4. The Mysteries: Each decade is dedicated to a specific mystery, inviting you to reflect on key events in the lives of Jesus and Mary.

How to Traditionally Pray the Rosary

Begin with the Sign of the Cross

Hold the crucifix and make the Sign of the Cross, touching your forehead as you say "In the name of the Father," your chest as you say "and of the Son," and your left and right shoulders as you say "and of the Holy Spirit. Amen.

Recite the Apostles' Creed

Still holding the crucifix, recite the Apostles' Creed as a profession of your faith: "I believe in God, the Father Almighty, Creator of heaven and earth, and in Jesus Christ, His only Son, our Lord, who was conceived by the Holy Spirit, born of the Virgin Mary, suffered under Pontius Pilate, was crucified, died, and was buried. He descended into hell; on the third day, He rose again from the dead; He ascended into heaven and is seated at the right hand of God, the Father Almighty; from there He will come to judge the living and the dead. I believe in the Holy Spirit, the Holy Catholic Church, the communion of saints, the forgiveness of sins, the resurrection of the body, and life everlasting. Amen."

For those who are not Catholic, this step can be omitted, or the prayer can be adapted to align with your own beliefs or spiritual practices.

Pray the Our Father

On the first large bead, pray the Our Father: "Our Father, who art in heaven, hallowed be Thy name. Thy kingdom come, Thy will be done, on earth as it is in heaven. Give us this day our daily bread, and forgive us our trespasses, as we forgive those who trespass against us. And lead us not into temptation, but deliver us from evil.*"

You may conclude with "Amen" here or, if you prefer, add the optional ending: "For Thine is the kingdom, and the power, and the glory, forever. Amen.

Pray the Hail Mary

On the next three smaller beads, pray three Hail Mary, traditionally for the virtues of faith, hope, and charity: "Hail Mary, full of grace, the Lord is with thee. Blessed art thou among women, and blessed is the fruit of thy womb, Jesus. Holy Mary, Mother of God, pray for us sinners, now and at the hour of our death. Amen."

Pray the Glory Be

On the next large bead, pray the Glory Be: "Glory be to the Father, and to the Son, and to the Holy Spirit, as it was in the beginning, is now, and ever shall be, world without end. Amen."

If you are Gnostic or follow another faith that embraces the sacred feminine, you can adapt this to honor the Holy Family, including the sacred feminine: Glory be to the Mother, the Father, and the Divine

Child, as it was in the beginning, is now, and ever shall be, world without end. Amen.

Announce the First Mystery

Before beginning the first decade, announce the mystery you will meditate on. For example: "The First Joyful Mystery: The Annunciation."

Pray the Decade

On the large bead, pray the Our Father. On each of the ten smaller beads, pray a Hail Mary. Conclude the decade with the Glory Be. (Optional: After the Glory Be, you may also pray the Fatima Prayer: "O my Jesus, forgive us our sins, save us from the fires of hell, and lead all souls to heaven, especially those in most need of Thy mercy.")

Repeat for All Five Mysteries Continue this pattern beginning at step 3 for all five decades, meditating on a different mystery for each.

Conclude with the Hail Holy Queen

Hail, Holy Queen, Mother of Mercy, our life, our sweetness, and our hope. To thee do we cry, poor banished children of Eve. To thee do we send up our sighs, mourning and weeping in this valley of tears. Turn then, most gracious advocate, thine eyes of mercy toward us, and after this, our exile, show unto us the blessed fruit of thy womb, Jesus. O clement, O loving, O sweet Virgin Mary. Pray for us, O Holy Mother of God, that we may be made worthy of the promises of Christ. Amen.

Closing Prayer

End with the Sign of the Cross and any additional prayers you feel called to offer, such as a litany, prayer of petition, or a personal devotion.

Reflecting on the Words of the Prayer and the Mysteries

During the Rosary, it is not only important to meditate on the mysteries but also to reflect deeply on the words of each prayer being recited. The prayers, especially the Hail Mary, hold rich spiritual and biblical significance that can deepen one's connection to the Blessed Virgin Mary. For example, as you pray the Hail Mary, consider the biblical events referenced in these words. "Hail, Mary, full of grace, the Lord is with thee," when the Angel Gabriel greeted Mary with these words (Luke 1:28). Reflect on the profound humility and trust displayed by Mary as she accepted God's plan for her. Similarly, "Blessed art thou among women, and blessed is the fruit of thy womb, Jesus," draws us to Elizabeth's greeting to Mary during the Visitation (Luke 1:42), a moment of joyous recognition of Jesus' presence.

This intentional reflection deepens your prayer and some have said makes you aware of Mary's presence, who is drawn closer to you in response to your plea: Holy Mary, Mother of God, Pray for Us.

5

The Mysteries of the Rosary

The Traditional Rosary is divided into four sets of mysteries, each focusing on significant events in the lives of Jesus and Mary. These mysteries are meditated upon during their respective decades, with each day of the week traditionally dedicated to a specific set:

Joyful Mysteries (Mondays and Saturdays)	Sorrowful Mysteries (Tuesdays and Fridays)	Glorious Mysteries (Wednesdays and Sundays)	Luminous Mysteries (Thursdays)
Annunciation	Agony in the Garden	Resurrection	Baptism of Jesus in the Jordan
Visitation	Scourging in the Pillar	Ascension	Wedding at Cana
Nativity	Crowning with Thorns	Descent of the Holy Spirit	Proclamation of the Kingdom
Presentation at the Temple	Carrying of the Cross	Assumption of Mary	Transfiguration
Finding of Jesus in the Temple	Crucifixion	Coronation of Mary	Institution of the Eucharist

Tips for a Meaningful Rosary Practice

1. Create a Sacred Space: Find a quiet place where you can pray without distractions. Light a candle or place an image of Mary nearby to create a sense of reverence.

2. Set an Intention: Before beginning, offer your Rosary for a specific intention, such as getting to know Mary and Jesus, healing, guidance, gratitude, etc.

3. Meditate on the Mysteries: As you pray each decade, visualize the mystery and reflect on its meaning in your life.

4. Pray Every Day: Praying the Rosary daily not only helps you memorize the prayers and structure but also connects you with a global community of people praying the same prayer on the same day. It's a beautiful way to feel united in faith. In addition, it improves your ability to focus and concentrate and even enter into the scenes of the decades with time.

5. Pray with Others: The Rosary is a powerful communal prayer. Consider praying with family, friends, or a local group.

6. Don't Treat the Rosary as Just a Petition Tool: The Rosary is more than a way to ask for favors. It's a tool for devotion, an offering of love, and an opportunity for deep reflection. Remember, the Rosary is not a magic wand, and praying it once doesn't guarantee immediate answers or profound changes. Instead, trust that the Rosary will bring about changes that will occur for you in divine time.

7. Be Patient with Yourself: If you're new to the Rosary, take your time learning the prayers and structure. The beauty of the Rosary lies in its simplicity and adaptability.

6

Understanding the Rosary's Prayers

The prayers of the Rosary are rich in meaning and tradition, offering a pathway to connect with God, Mary, and the mysteries of faith. Each prayer carries profound spiritual significance, and its interpretation can vary across different theological perspectives. In this chapter, we will explore the Catholic, Gnostic, and Pentecostal interpretations of the key prayers of the Rosary.

The Apostle's Creed

> " I believe in God, the Father almighty, creator of heaven and earth. I believe in Jesus Christ, his only Son, our Lord, who was conceived by the Holy Spirit and born of the virgin Mary. He suffered under Pontius Pilate, was crucified, died, and was buried; he descended to hell. The third day he rose again from the dead. He ascended to heaven and is seated at the right hand of God the Father almighty. From there he will come to judge the living and the dead. I believe in the Holy Spirit, the holy Catholic church, the communion of saints, the forgiveness of sins, the resurrection of the body, and life everlasting. Amen."

Traditional Catholic Interpretation

The Apostle's Creed is a profession of faith, summarizing the core beliefs of Christianity. It affirms the Trinity, the life and mission of Jesus Christ, the role of the Church, and the hope of eternal life. Catholics recite this prayer to declare their faith and align themselves with the teachings of the Church.

Gnostic Interpretation

In Gnostic thought, the Apostle's Creed is seen as a symbolic journey of the soul. God the Father represents the divine source within, the eternal "I AM." Jesus Christ symbolizes the awakened imagination and the path to spiritual enlightenment. The Virgin Mary represents the purity of the soul, untainted by material corruption. The resurrection is understood as the soul's liberation from the material world and its return to divine unity.

Pentecostal Interpretation

For Pentecostals, the Apostle's Creed is a declaration of faith in the power of the Holy Spirit and the living presence of Jesus Christ. It emphasizes the transformative power of salvation, the authority of Scripture, and the hope of the Second Coming. The Creed is a reminder of God's active role in the believer's life.

The Glory Be

> "Glory be to the Father
> and to the Son
> and to the Holy Spirit,
> as it was in the beginning
> is now, and ever shall be
> world without end. Amen."

Traditional Catholic Interpretation

The Glory Be is a doxology, a short hymn of praise to the Holy Trinity. It acknowledges God's eternal nature and invites the faithful to glorify Him in all things.

Gnostic Interpretation

In Gnostic thought, the Glory Be reflects the divine aspects within the self:

- The Father is the conscious awareness of the divine.

- The Son is the manifestation of divine will in the material world.

- The Holy Spirit is the bridge between the spiritual and material realms, the force that brings divine ideas into reality.

The phrase "world without end" symbolizes the infinite potential of consciousness, and "Amen" is the affirmation of divine truth.

Pentecostal Interpretation

For Pentecostals, the Glory Be is a heartfelt expression of worship and gratitude to the Trinity. It is a reminder of God's unchanging nature and His eternal presence in the believer's life. The prayer is often accompanied by spontaneous praise and thanksgiving.

The Our Father

> "Our Father, Who art in heaven,
> Hallowed be Thy Name.
> Thy Kingdom come.
> Thy Will be done,
> on earth as it is in Heaven. Give us this day our daily bread.
> And forgive us our trespasses,
> as we forgive those who trespass against us.
> And lead us not into temptation,
> but deliver us from evil. Amen."

Traditional Catholic Interpretation

The Our Father, or the Lord's Prayer, is the prayer Jesus taught His disciples. It is a model of prayer that encompasses praise, petition, and surrender to God's will. Catholics see it as a perfect prayer that aligns the heart with God's desires. A minority of Catholics interpret the "daily bread" as a nod to The Eucharist.

Gnostic Interpretation

In Gnostic thought, the Our Father is a meditation on the divine within:

- "Our Father who art in heaven" acknowledges the divine source within the higher self.

- "Thy kingdom come" is a call to manifest divine truth in the material world.

- "Give us this day our daily bread" symbolizes spiritual nourishment and enlightenment.

- "Deliver us from evil" is a plea to transcend ignorance and material attachments.

Pentecostal Interpretation

For Pentecostals, the Our Father is a powerful prayer of faith and dependence on God. It is often prayed with fervor, emphasizing God's provision, protection, and guidance. The prayer is seen as a declaration of trust in God's sovereignty.

The Hail Mary

> "Hail, Mary, full of grace,
> the Lord is with thee.
> Blessed art thou amongst women
> and blessed is the fruit of thy womb, Jesus.
> Holy Mary, Mother of God,
> pray for us sinners,
> now and at the hour of our death.
> Amen."

Traditional Catholic Interpretation

The Hail Mary is a prayer of veneration to Mary, the Mother of God. It acknowledges her role in salvation history and seeks her intercession. Key lines of the prayer are taken directly from the Bible, such as "Hail, full of grace, the Lord is with you" (Luke 1:28) and "Blessed are you among women, and blessed is the fruit of your womb" (Luke 1:42). "Pray for us Sinners, Now and at the Hour of Our Death" is also seen as an intercessory prayer by psychopomps and acknowledgement of Mary's role as literally providing her faithful with a peaceful passing.

Gnostic Interpretation

In both Gnostic thought and Neville Goddard's metaphysical interpretation, the "Hail Mary" prayer is seen as a profound acknowledgment of spiritual principles, focusing on the creative and transformative power within us:

"Hail Mary, full of grace, the Lord is with thee":

- Gnostics honor the purity and wisdom of the soul as the vessel for divine truth.

- Neville interprets Mary as the subconscious mind, filled with infinite potential ("full of grace") and always connected to the I AM presence ("the Lord is with thee").

- It is through honoring this subconscious creative force that manifestations begin.

"Blessed art thou among women, and blessed is the fruit of thy womb, Jesus":

- Gnostics see this as acknowledging the soul's unique role in manifesting divine truth.

- Neville teaches that the "womb" symbolizes the subconscious as the birther of manifestations. Among all possible states (women), the chosen belief ("Mary") gives life to the desired outcome ("Jesus"), which is the fruit of the subconscious impression.

"Holy Mary, Mother of God, pray for us sinners":

- For Gnostics, this is a call to align with divine wisdom and transcend ignorance.

- Neville defines "Mary" as the subconscious, the "Mother of God" (I AM), working to materialize assumptions. "Sinners" are those disconnected from divine alignment, and prayer is seen as aligning the subconscious with higher truth.

"Now and at the hour of our death. Amen":

- Gnostics emphasize the present moment as key to awakening divine wisdom.

- Neville interprets this as the present moment ("now") being the gateway to transformation. "The hour of our death" symbolizes letting go of old states of consciousness, and "Amen" seals the new assumption as a command for realization.

Ultimately, both perspectives highlight the transformative power of aligning with divine truth, whether through honoring the soul's wisdom or by consciously impressing the subconscious mind with desired states. The "Hail Mary" becomes a tool for manifesting higher truths and bringing desires into reality.

Pentecostal Interpretation

Pentecostals typically do not pray the Hail Mary, as they focus on direct prayer to God through Jesus Christ. However, they may honor Mary as a faithful servant of God and an example of obedience and faith.

The Fatima Prayer

> "O My Jesus, forgive us our sins, save us from the fires of Hell and lead all souls to Heaven, especially those who are in most need of Thy mercy."

Traditional Catholic Interpretation

The Fatima Prayer was revealed during the apparitions of Mary at Fatima. It is a plea for mercy and the salvation of souls, reflecting the urgency of prayer and repentance.

Gnostic Interpretation

In Gnostic thought, the Fatima Prayer is a call to awaken the divine spark within and to seek liberation from ignorance. The plea for mercy is understood as a desire for spiritual enlightenment and unity with the divine.

Pentecostal Interpretation

Pentecostals may not use the Fatima Prayer, but they share its emphasis on repentance and the salvation of souls. They often pray for revival and the outpouring of the Holy Spirit to bring transformation and healing.

The Hail Holy Queen

> "Hail, holy Queen, Mother of mercy, hail, our life, our sweetness and our hope. To thee do we cry, poor banished children of Eve: to thee do we send up our sighs, mourning and weeping in this vale of tears. Turn then, most gracious Advocate, thine eyes of mercy toward us, and after this our exile, show unto us the blessed fruit of thy womb, Jesus, O merciful, O loving, O sweet Virgin Mary! Amen."

Traditional Catholic Interpretation

The Hail Holy Queen is a prayer of devotion to Mary, seeking her intercession and guidance. It acknowledges her as the Mother of Mercy and a source of hope for the faithful.

Gnostic Interpretation

In Gnostic thought, the "Hail Holy Queen" is revered as a hymn to the Divine Feminine, embodying the nurturing and compassionate aspect of the divine. It symbolizes the soul's journey toward enlightenment and the guidance of divine wisdom. Christian mystics like Neville Goddard offer a metaphysical interpretation of this prayer, framing it as a conversation with one's own consciousness and creative power. Neville taught that all prayers are directed toward the subconscious mind, the "Holy Queen" that manifests our reality. Here's how he might decode the symbolism of the "Hail Holy Queen" within this framework:

"Hail, Holy Queen, Mother of Mercy":

- The "Holy Queen" represents the subconscious mind, the ruler of our manifested world.

- The "Mother of Mercy" signifies the creative womb of imagination that nurtures and births compassionate outcomes.

Key Insight: We are addressing our inner creative power, the subconscious, which governs our lives.

"Our life, our sweetness, and our hope":

- "Life" reflects the state of consciousness you currently inhabit.

- "Sweetness and hope" symbolize the joyful fulfillment of desires when assumed as real.

Key Insight: The subconscious is the source of fulfillment and the certainty of manifestation.

"To thee do we cry, poor banished children of Eve" :

- "Children of Eve" refers to humanity believing in separation from God. "Exile" reflects disconnection from the divine self (the "I AM").

Key Insight: We cry out to our higher awareness, seeking rescue from limiting beliefs and false perceptions.

"Mourning and weeping in this valley of tears":

- The "valley of tears" signifies the struggles of the 3D world, which reflect unfulfilled desires.

Key Insight: The outer world reflects the inner state. When the subconscious is barren of fulfillment, this is mirrored as struggle.

"Turn then, most gracious advocate, thine eyes of mercy toward us" :

- The "advocate" is the subconscious mind interceding on our behalf.

- "Eyes of mercy" suggest a shift in perception, focusing on fulfillment rather than lack.

Key Insight: By engaging the imagination with belief, the subconscious can manifest our desires.

"Show unto us the blessed fruit of thy womb, Jesus" :

- The "fruit of thy womb" symbolizes the desires made real through persistent assumption.

- "After this our exile" refers to the end of identifying with lack and stepping into fulfillment.

Key Insight: The "Jesus" within us-our fulfilled desires-is birthed when we embody the feeling of the wish fulfilled.

"O clement, O loving, O sweet Virgin Mary":

- These attributes reflect the nature of the subconscious, which always yields to dominant assumptions.

Key Insight: The subconscious is ever-ready to respond with "yes" to the visions we impress upon it.

Pentecostal Interpretation

Pentecostals do not typically pray the Hail Holy Queen, but they may honor Mary as a model of faith and obedience. They focus on direct prayer to God and the work of the Holy Spirit in their lives.

7

Understanding the Traditional Mysteries

The Rosary is more than a reflection on the lives of Jesus and Mary- it's an invitation to discover deeper truths about ourselves. Each of the traditional mysteries, divided into four sets, highlights significant events in their lives, but these stories go beyond mere reflection. As we meditate on each mystery, we are encouraged to consider how these events mirror our own joys, struggles, and faith. They prompt us to ask meaningful questions: How do these moments relate to my life? What grace can I seek to transform my challenges into growth? Through this prayerful journey, the Rosary becomes a tool for personal transformation, helping us uncover new insights, deepen our faith, and connect more fully with our own spiritual path.

The traditional Rosary is a treasure trove of spiritual knowledge, intricately crafted to guide our hearts and minds toward profound truths. Its structure is not random but deeply intentional, aligning specific mysteries with particular days of the week to help us meditate on the life of Christ and the Virgin Mary in an ordered and meaningful way.

Each bead, each prayer, and each sequence invites us to pause and reflect, offering countless opportunities for growth and understanding. What follows are reflections and guiding questions designed to accompany you as you meditate on the traditional mysteries. These are meant to deepen your prayer experience, helping you to uncover personal insights and connect more intimately with the timeless wisdom embedded within the Rosary.

The Joyful Mysteries

1. The Annunciation

"Behold, I am the handmaid of the Lord; let it be to me according to your word."(Luke 1:26-38)

Reflection: Reflect on Mary's "yes" to God's plan and ask for the grace to trust in divine guidance, even when the path is unclear.

General Question: Where in my life am I saying "yes" to God? Where in my life am I asking God, "How?"

Gnostic Reflection: Symbolizing the moment you accept your desire as a possibility. Imagination as the divine seed planted within the subconscious.

Gnostic Question: Where in my life am I planting the divine seed of imagination? How can I nurture this possibility into belief?

2. The Visitation

"Blessed are you among women, and blessed is the fruit of your womb!"(Luke 1:39-56)

Reflection: Consider the joy of sharing God's blessings with others and pray for a heart open to service and compassion.

General Question: How can I share God's blessings with others today? Who in my life needs my compassion and service?

Gnostic Reflection: Sharing your vision with others or affirming it within yourself. The subconscious begins to nurture and grow your desire.

Gnostic Question: How can I affirm my vision to myself or with others? What steps am I taking to nurture my desire into growth?

3. The Nativity

"And she gave birth to her firstborn son and wrapped him in swaddling cloths and laid him in a manger."(Luke 2:1-20)

Reflection: Meditate on the humility of Christ's birth and the gift of God's presence in our lives.

General Question: Where do I see God's presence in my life? How can I embrace humility?

Gnostic Reflection: The birth of your desire into the physical world. Manifestation as the result of unwavering faith and inner alignment.

Gnostic Question: What desire has been birthed into my life through faith? How can I align more fully with my inner vision?

4. The Presentation in the Temple

"My eyes have seen your salvation."(Luke 2:22-38)

Reflection: Reflect on the act of offering your life and loved ones to God, trusting in His plan.

General Question: What areas of my life do I need to surrender to God? How can I trust more fully in His plan?

Gnostic Reflection: Offering up your manifestation to the divine. A reflection of gratitude and acknowledgment of the creative process.

Gnostic Question: How can I express gratitude for the creative process? What part of my manifestation do I offer back to the divine?

5. The Finding of Jesus in the Temple

"Did you not know that I must be in my Father's house?"
(Luke 2:41-50)

Reflection: Pray for the wisdom to seek God in all things and to trust in His timing.

General Question: Where am I seeking God in my daily life? How can I grow in trust when His plans seem unclear?

Gnostic Reflection: Rediscovering the Christ within-your imagination as the true source of creation.

Gnostic Question: How can I reconnect with my inner divine imagination? Where have I overlooked the creative power within me?

Sorrowful Mysteries

1. The Agony in the Garden

"Father, if you are willing, take this cup from me; yet not my will, but yours be done." (Luke 22:42)

Reflection: Reflect on the moments of trial in your life, asking for the grace to surrender to God's divine will, even in times of suffering and uncertainty.

General Question: How can I trust more deeply in God during moments of personal agony or despair?

Gnostic Reflection: Contemplate the inner conflict between fear and faith, awakening to the divine strength within to face challenges courageously.

Gnostic Question: How can I quiet the inner turmoil to connect with the higher wisdom within me?

2. The Scourging at the Pillar

"Then Pilate took Jesus and had Him flogged." (John 19:1)

Reflection: Meditate on Christ's suffering and sacrifice, offering up your own pain in union with His for the redemption of the world.

General Question: Where in my life can I offer my struggles to bring about healing and transformation?

Gnostic Reflection: See this as a symbol of purification, stripping away attachments to reveal the divine essence beneath.

Gnostic Question: How can I see my own pain as a path to inner purification and growth?

3. The Crowning with Thorns

> "They clothed Him in a purple robe and went up to Him again and again, saying, 'Hail, king of the Jews!' And they slapped Him in the face." (John 19:2-3)

Reflection: Consider the humiliation and mockery Christ endured, and invite God to help you cultivate humility and patience in the face of adversity.

General Question: How can I grow in humility when faced with criticism or rejection?

Gnostic Reflection: Recognize this as the transcendence of ego, affirming the light of the divine self beyond worldly scorn.

Gnostic Question: How can I transcend the limitations of my ego to live from a place of divine purpose?

4. The Carrying of the Cross

> "Whoever wants to be my disciple must deny themselves and take up their cross daily and follow me." (Luke 9:23)

Reflection: Reflect on your personal crosses and how you can carry them with love and perseverance, trusting in God's strength to help you.

General Question: What "cross" am I being invited to carry, and how can I do so with faith and grace?

Gnostic Reflection: Ponder the symbolic weight of the cross as the burdens of duality, inviting the divine within to bring balance and unity.

Gnostic Question: How can I bring balance to my inner struggles and align with my divine essence?

5. The Crucifixion and Death of Jesus

"Father, into your hands I commit my spirit." (Luke 23:46)

Reflection: Contemplate the depth of Christ's love for humanity and His ultimate sacrifice. Offer yourself fully to God's plan, letting go of what holds you back.

General Question: How can I surrender more fully to God's will in my life?

Gnostic Reflection: See the crucifixion as the ultimate symbol of letting go of the material self to awaken to resurrection and divine life.

Gnostic Question: What parts of my false self am I being called to release to experience spiritual rebirth?

Glorious Mysteries

1. The Resurrection

"He is not here; He has risen, just as He said." (Matthew 28:6)

Reflection: Rejoice in the victory of Christ over death and find renewed hope and faith in His promise of eternal life.

General Question: How can I live each day in the hope and joy of Christ's resurrection?

Gnostic Reflection: Celebrate the awakening of the higher self and the triumph of light over darkness within your own being.

Gnostic Question: How can I awaken to the radiant light of my inner divine self?

2. The Ascension

"He was taken up before their very eyes, and a cloud hid Him from their sight." (Acts 1:9)

Reflection: Reflect on Christ's ascension as a call to set your heart on heavenly things and trust that He is always with you.

General Question: How can I focus my mind and heart on spiritual things amidst the distractions of daily life?

Gnostic Reflection: See the ascension as a metaphor for rising above worldly attachments, aligning with the divine within.

Gnostic Question: What worldly attachments am I being invited to release to ascend to a higher spiritual state?

3. The Descent of the Holy Spirit

> "They saw what seemed to be tongues of fire that separated and came to rest on each of them. All of them were filled with the Holy Spirit." (Acts 2:3-4)

Reflection: Reflect on the gift of the Holy Spirit, who empowers and guides us to live out our faith boldly and with love.

General Question: How can I invite the Holy Spirit into my daily life to guide my actions and decisions?

Gnostic Reflection: See the descent of the Holy Spirit as a call to awaken the divine spark within, allowing wisdom and intuition to guide your spiritual path.

Gnostic Question: How can I nurture the divine spark within me to live a life of greater consciousness and love?

4. The Assumption of Mary

> "The queen stands at your right hand, arrayed in gold." (Psalm 45:9)

Reflection: Consider Mary's assumption into heaven as a reminder of the promise of eternal life for those who live faithfully.

General Question: How can I align my daily choices with the hope and promise of eternal life?

Gnostic Reflection: Contemplate Mary's assumption as an allegory for the soul's ascension towards divine union. Reflect on how the soul, when freed from the physical constraints of the material world, can ascend to its spiritual origin, seeking harmony and wholeness. This can inspire a deeper pursuit of self-knowledge and a connection with the divine spark within.

Gnostic Question: What practices and insights can help liberate my soul from earthly attachments and guide it toward divine fulfillment?

5. The Coronation of Mary

> "A great sign appeared in heaven: a woman clothed with the sun, with the moon under her feet and a crown of twelve stars on her head." (Revelation 12:1)

Reflection: Reflect on Mary's coronation as Queen of Heaven and Earth, symbolizing the fulfillment of God's promises and the glory awaiting the faithful.

General Question: How does Mary's coronation inspire us to trust in God's plan and strive for holiness in our daily lives?

Gnostic Reflection: Ponder Mary's coronation as a representation of the ultimate union of the soul with divine wisdom, crowned in eternal love and light.

Gnostic Question: How does Mary's crowning reflect the soul's ascent and its ultimate harmony with the divine light and truth?

Luminous Mysteries

1. The Baptism of Jesus in the Jordan

> "And when Jesus was baptized, immediately he went up from the water, and behold, the heavens were opened to him." (Matthew 3:16)

Reflection: Jesus' baptism invites us to renew our own baptismal promises and recognize our identity as beloved children of God.

General Question: How can I live each day with the awareness that I am a beloved child of God?

Gnostic Reflection: Contemplate the baptism as a metaphor for awakening the divine within, cleansing the soul to perceive higher realities.

Gnostic Question: What aspects of my inner self need to be purified to uncover the divine spark within me?

2. The Wedding at Cana

> "His mother said to the servants, 'Do whatever he tells you.'" (John 2:5)

Reflection: The transformation of water into wine at Cana reminds us of God's abundant blessings and the trust we should place in His will.

General Question: How can I trust more deeply in God's providence and allow His will to guide my actions?

Gnostic Reflection: Meditate on the Wedding at Cana as a symbol of the alchemical process of spiritual transformation, turning the ordinary into the extraordinary.

Gnostic Question: What aspects of my spiritual being need transformation to align with the divine essence within me?

3. The Proclamation of the Kingdom

> "Jesus went throughout Galilee, teaching in their synagogues, proclaiming the good news of the kingdom, and healing every disease and sickness among the people."(Matthew 4:23)

Reflection: Through His proclamation of the Kingdom, Jesus invites us to repentance, renewal, and a deeper relationship with God. His words and miracles remind us of the hope and joy found in living according to the Gospel.

General Question: How can I better live out the values of the Kingdom of God in my daily life? Gnostic Reflection: Reflect on the Kingdom of God as the awakening of divine consciousness within, a realm not of this world but of the soul's eternal truth. Seek spiritual insight to embody Christ's teachings fully within your inner being.

Gnostic Question: What steps can I take to awaken the divine presence within me and act with greater spiritual awareness?

4. The Transfiguration

> "As he was praying, the appearance of his face changed, and his clothes became as bright as a flash of lightning (Luke 9:29)

Reflection: The Transfiguration reveals Jesus in His divine glory, strengthening the faith of His disciples and offering a glimpse of the eternal life promised to us. It is a moment of awe that calls us to listen to and follow Him wholeheartedly.

General Question: How can I be more attentive to God's presence in my life and grow in faith through challenging times?

Gnostic Reflection: Contemplate the Transfiguration as the unveiling of divine light within. Recognize moments of spiritual insight as glimpses of your true nature, illuminated by God's grace.

Gnostic Question: What practices help me to reveal the divine light within and align myself with God's truth?

5. The Institution of the Eucharist

> "Then he took a cup, and when he had given thanks, he gave it to them, saying, 'Drink from it, all of you. This is my blood of the covenant, which is poured out for many for the forgiveness of sins.'" (Matthew 26:27-28)

Reflection: The institution of the Eucharist is the ultimate gift of Christ's love, offering His very body and blood for the salvation of humanity. It reminds us of the depth of His sacrifice and calls us to unity with Him and one another.

General Question: How can I deepen my relationship with Christ through the gift of the Eucharist?

Gnostic Reflection: Consider the Eucharist as a mystical union, where the physical and spiritual intertwine. Contemplate this sacrament as a reflection of the sacred exchange between the divine and the human soul.

Gnostic Question: How does reflecting on the Eucharist inspire me to seek unity between my earthly actions and my spiritual essence?

The Seven Sorrows of Mary

The Seven Sorrows Rosary, also known as the Servite Rosary, focuses on the sorrowful events in Mary's life. It was popularized by the Servite Order in the 13th century and is prayed on a special rosary with seven sets of seven beads.

1. The Prophecy of Simeon

> "Behold, this child is appointed for the fall and rising of many in Israel, and for a sign that is opposed (and a sword will pierce through your own soul also), so that thoughts from many hearts may be revealed." (Luke 2:34-35)

Reflection: Pray for the grace to accept God's will, even when it brings sorrow.

Question for reflection: How do I respond to the unexpected sorrows in my life, and do I trust in God's greater plan?

Gnostic perspective: This is the first shock of awakening-when you realize the path of wisdom is also one of grief.

2. The Flight into Egypt

> "Rise, take the child and his mother, and flee to Egypt, and remain there until I tell you, for Herod is about to search for the child, to destroy him." (Matthew 2:13)

Reflection: Reflect on Mary's trust in God's protection during times of uncertainty.

Question for reflection: How do I trust God's guidance when I feel lost or afraid?

Gnostic perspective: The flight into Egypt signifies the need to flee from ignorance and spiritual danger. In addition, the Divine Feminine always survives the empire's violence but at great cost.

3. The Loss of the Child Jesus in the Temple

> "After three days they found him in the temple, sitting among the teachers, listening to them and asking them questions." (Luke 2:46)

Reflection: Pray for the grace to seek God when He feels distant.

Question for reflection: When I feel distant from God, do I actively seek Him or become discouraged?

Gnostic perspective: The loss of Jesus symbolizes the soul's struggle to reconnect with divine wisdom. The search through the temple represents the Gnostic's pursuit of hidden knowledge within the sacred teachings. Finally, it represents the dark night of the soul-when even the Christ within feels absent.

4. Mary Meets Jesus on the Way to Calvary

> "And there followed him a great multitude of the people and of women who were mourning and lamenting for him." (Luke 23:27)

Reflection: Reflect on Mary's strength and pray for the courage to accompany others in their suffering.

Question for reflection: How can I stand alongside others in their suffering with compassion and courage?

Gnostic perspective: This encounter represents the soul's recognition of the suffering inherent in the material world. Mary's strength teaches Gnostics to endure the pain of this existence while staying true to the higher spiritual path. In addition, this is the moment you witness your own divinity being crucified by the world.

5. The Crucifixion and Death of Jesus

> "When Jesus saw his mother and the disciple whom he loved standing nearby, he said to his mother, 'Woman, behold, your son!'" (John 19:26)

Reflection: Meditate on Mary's sorrow at the foot of the cross and pray for the grace to unite your suffering with Christ's.

Question for reflection: How can I offer my pain and struggles in union with God's redemptive work?

Gnostic perspective: The crucifixion symbolizes the ultimate sacrifice to transcend material limitations. For Gnostics, it represents the liberation of the divine spark from the confines of the flesh, pointing the way to spiritual awakening. The death of the ego-the illusion that God is "out there" and not within.

6. The Body of Jesus is Taken Down from the Cross

> "Then he took it down and wrapped it in a linen shroud and laid him in a tomb cut in stone, where no one had ever yet been laid." (Luke 23:53)

Reflection: Pray for the grace to find peace in moments of loss.

Question for reflection: How can I find peace and hope even in the midst of loss? Gnostic perspective: This moment signifies the soul's preparation for transformation. For Gnostics, it represents the laying aside of the physical body to focus on the eternal and spiritual nature of existence. The alchemy of grief-holding what was lost until it transforms.

7. The Burial of Jesus

"The women who had come with him from Galilee followed and saw the tomb and how his body was laid. Then they returned and prepared spices and ointments." (Luke 23:55-56)

Reflection: Reflect on Mary's hope in the resurrection and pray for the grace to trust in God's promises.

Question for reflection: How can I remain hopeful and trust in God's promises even when things feel hopeless?

Gnostic perspective: The burial represents the soul's entry into the mystery of death and rebirth. For Gnostics, it is a reminder of the promise of spiritual resurrection and liberation from the material world through divine knowledge. This is the final surrender- the dark womb before rebirth.

Promises of the Seven Sorrows Rosary

Those who have a devotion to the Seven Sorrows Rosary are promised seven special graces, as revealed by the Blessed Virgin Mary:

1. I will bring peace to their families.

2. They will gain an understanding of divine mysteries.

3. I will comfort them in their sufferings and support them in their work.

4. I will grant them what they ask for, as long as it aligns with the will of my divine Son and the sanctification of their souls.

5. I will protect them in spiritual battles against the infernal enemy and guard them throughout their lives.

6. I will assist them visibly at the hour of their death, allowing them to see the face of their Mother.

7. I have obtained from my divine Son the grace that those who spread this devotion to my tears and sorrows will pass directly from this earthly life to eternal happiness, with all their sins forgiven, and my Son and I will be their everlasting comfort and joy.

The Seven Joys of Mary

The Seven Joys Rosary, or Franciscan Crown, celebrates joyful events in Mary's life and originated with the Franciscans in the 15th century. Its history traces back to a young Franciscan novice who honored Mary by offering flowers to her statue. Mary appeared to him, suggesting he honor her joys through prayer instead. Inspired, he structured a rosary around seven key moments of joy in Mary's life, creating the Franciscan Crown Rosary, a rosary with seven decades.

1. The Annunciation

"The angel Gabriel was sent from God to a town of Galilee called Nazareth, to a virgin betrothed to a man named Joseph."(Luke 1:26-38)

Reflection: Mary's "yes" to God's plan reminds us of the power of surrender and trust in divine will.

Questions for Reflection: Am I open to saying "yes" to the unexpected plans God has for our lives? What is something that God is trusting me with?

Gnostic Perspective: The Annunciation symbolizes the awakening of divine knowledge within the soul, where the inner Christ consciousness begins to take form. This is the moment your Higher Self whispers: "You are chosen-to embody the Divine.

2. The Visitation

> "When Elizabeth heard Mary's greeting, the infant leaped in her womb, and Elizabeth, filled with the Holy Spirit, cried out in a loud voice." (Luke 1:39-56)

Reflection: The bond between Mary and Elizabeth shows the beauty of spiritual community and shared joy.

Questions for Reflection: How can I be a source of encouragement and joy in the lives of those around me? How can I support others as they embrace God's work in their lives?

Gnostic Perspective: The Visitation represents the recognition of divinity in others, as Elizabeth symbolizes the awakened soul acknowledging the presence of divine wisdom.

3. The Nativity

> "And she gave birth to her firstborn son. She wrapped him in swaddling clothes and laid him in a manger."(Luke 2:1-20)

Reflection: Jesus' humble birth in a stable teaches us that greatness is often found in simplicity.

Questions for Reflection: Do we recognize humble beginnings as opportunities for divine grace? Can I appreciate when life unfolds in ways that I don't expect?

Gnostic Perspective: The Nativity signifies the birth of the inner Christ within the soul, bringing light and wisdom into the material world.

4. The Adoration of the Magi

"They were overjoyed at seeing the star, and on entering the house, they saw the child with Mary, his mother."(Matthew 2:1-12)

Reflection: The Magi's journey reminds us to seek truth and adore God's presence in our lives.

Question for Reflection: What is the "star" guiding me toward truth, and how can I follow it with faith and dedication?

Gnostic Perspective: This event reflects the acknowledgment of divine knowledge by the wise, symbolizing a soul's journey toward enlightenment and higher understanding.

5. The Finding of Jesus in the Temple

"After three days they found him in the temple, sitting in the midst of the teachers, listening to them and asking them questions." (Luke 2:41-50)

Reflection: Even in moments of confusion, Jesus shows us the importance of being in our Father's house.

Question for Reflection: Where am I searching for God's wisdom, and how can I better seek His presence in my daily life?

Gnostic Perspective: This moment represents the rediscovery of divine truth within ourselves, as the temple signifies the inner sanctuary where divine wisdom resides. It also represents your ability to see dogma-not to obey, but to outwit the keepers of lies.

6. The Resurrection

"Why do you seek the living among the dead? He is not here, but he has been raised." (Luke 24:1-12)

Reflection: The Resurrection offers hope and renewal, reminding us of the victory over sin and death.

Questions for Reflection: How can we embrace the joy of resurrection in my own life? What areas of my life need renewal?

Gnostic Perspective: The Resurrection symbolizes the awakening of spiritual consciousness, transcending the limitations of the material world to achieve unity with the divine.

7. The Assumption and Coronation of Mary

(No direct scripture reference, though it is rooted in sacred tradition.)

Reflection: Mary's Assumption inspires us to look toward heaven and trust in God's promise of eternal life.

Question for Reflection: How can I grow in faith and hope, trusting in God's promise of eternal life?

Gnostic Perspective: The Assumption represents the ascension of the soul into unity with the divine, showing the potential for spiritual transcendence and enlightenment.

Promises of the 7 Joys of Mary Rosary

Devotion to the 7 Joys of Mary Rosary, also known as the Franciscan Crown Rosary, is accompanied by profound promises, indulgences, and spiritual graces. Those who recite this rosary with genuine faith and devotion can expect a deepening of their relationship with the Blessed Virgin Mary and an increased awareness of her intercessory power.

Specific indulgences have been granted by the Church for its recitation, particularly by friars of the Franciscan Order and the faithful who honor Mary's joys. Graces include consolation in times of distress, growth in humility, and the strengthening of faith and hope in God's promises.

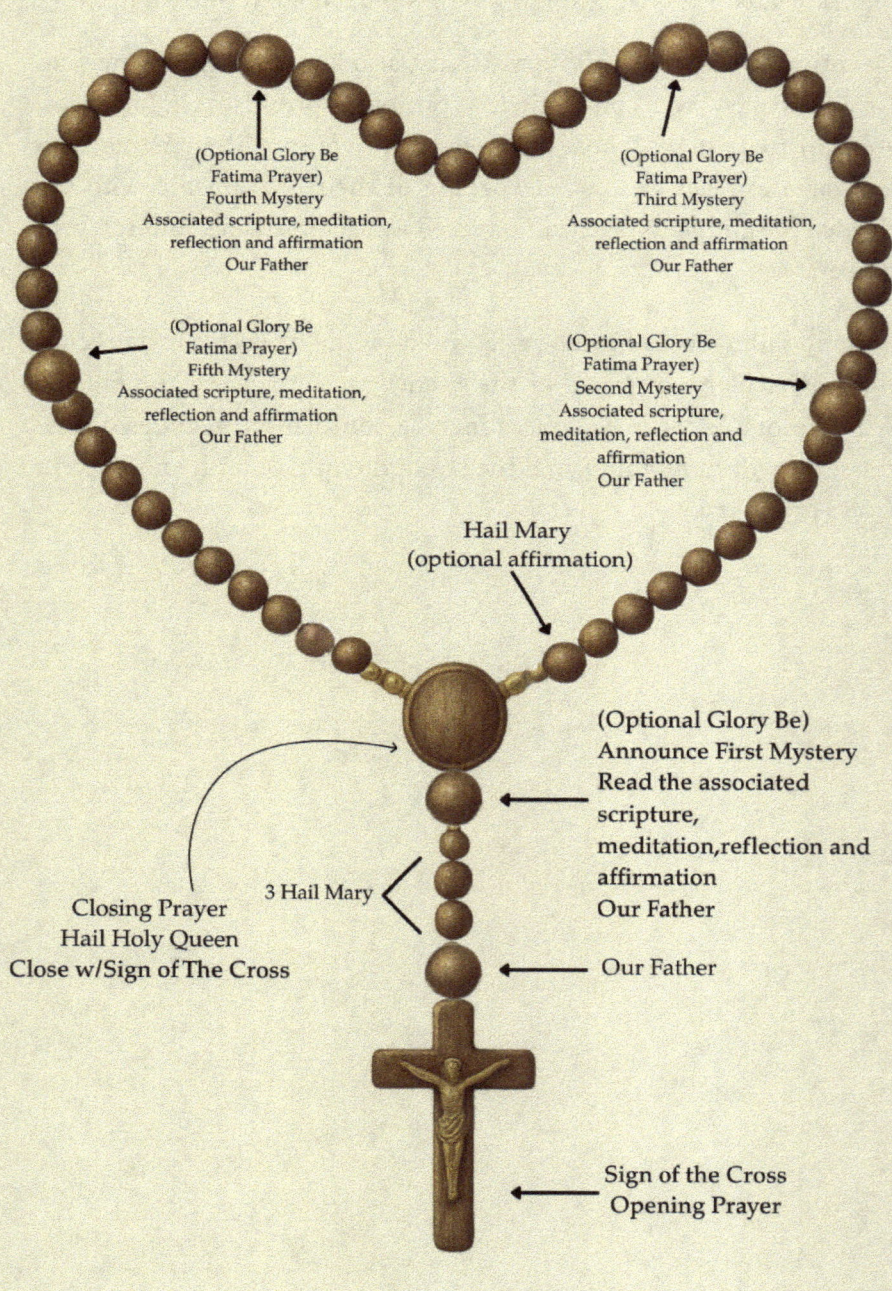

8

How to Pray Through Modern Mysteries

The Rosary is a living prayer, one that evolves with the needs of the faithful and the challenges of the times. While the traditional mysteries guide us through the life of Jesus and Mary, these new mysteries invite us to reflect on modern-day themes while also deepening our connection to other biblical characters. They are designed to resonate with the struggles and hopes of today, offering a sacred space for reflection, prayer, and transformation.

Each of these mysteries is rooted in scripture, Catholic tradition, or even Gnostic texts, and paired with meditations and affirmations that speak to the heart of contemporary life. As you pray these mysteries, allow Mary's presence to guide you, offering her wisdom, grace, and strength for the journey.

To pray these mysteries, begin by announcing the specific mystery and reflecting on its theme. If scripture is associated with the mystery, take a moment to read or meditate on the passage, allowing it to resonate in your heart. Then read the meditation and affirmation. This book offers meditations for each of the decades, providing reflections and insights to guide your prayer and deepen your understanding of the mysteries. However, you are encouraged to be inspired and to meditate on the aspect of the mystery that resonates most deeply with you in the moment. Whether it's a particular word within the scriptural passage, a personal intention, or a new realization, you are free to focus on what feels most pertinent to your spiritual journey.

Afterward, pray 1 Our Father, focusing on the intentions held within the mystery. Then, proceed with 10 Hail Marys, or the associated affirmations if you feel called- letting the rhythm of the prayer guide you deeper into contemplation. You are advised to take your time with these prayers and allow for silence so that you can hear the messages that these mysteries have for you. With each Hail Mary bead, allow your heart to be attuned to the grace and inspiration of the mystery, welcoming whatever spiritual insights or feelings may unfold as you pray.

Finally, conclude with 1 Glory Be. Repeat this process for each of the mysteries.

9

Rosaries for Modern Day Issues

"Learn to do right; seek justice. Defend the oppressed."
(Isaiah 1:17)

The world today is marked by a range of complex and urgent challenges that demand both moral clarity and action. Issues such as immigration, economic inequality, climate change, and the rise of artificial intelligence present profound ethical dilemmas that shape our future. At the same time, the fight against racism and the call for accountable leadership require deep reflection, courage,and a commitment to unity. These challenges can feel overwhelming, often leaving us searching for guidance and strength to respond with both compassion and purpose.

Rosaries can serve as a tool for meditation and prayer in these moments, offering a path to spiritual grounding and solidarity. They invite us to reflect on faith, hope, and the responsibility we have to foster justice, care for creation, and uphold the dignity of every person. The following rosaries are designed to guide you in addressing these modern-day issues. Through prayerful reflection, they provide a framework for navigating difficult questions, seeking wisdom, and finding the courage to act with integrity and love in the face of the challenges that define our times.

Living in Fear of Political Oppression

For courage, trust in God's providence, and solidarity with the oppressed

Opening Prayer

O Our Lady of Perpetual Help, Wrap us in your mantle of protection during uncertain times. Intercede for all who live under fear and injustice.

Comfort the persecuted, grant wisdom to the oppressed, courage to the righteous, and mercy to the powerful.

As you fled tyranny with your Son, help us trust in God's justice even in exile. Amen.

1st Mystery: The Tyranny of Herod

"When Herod realized that he had been outwitted by the Magi, he was furious, and he gave orders to kill all the boys in Bethlehem." (Matthew 2:16)

Meditation: Jesus was born into a violent, unstable world. Even as a baby, he threatened corrupt power. The Divine often challenges those in control, representing truth and freedom.

Reflection: When I feel powerless before injustice, can I trust that God is still guiding and intervening in silence?

Affirmation: "I trust that no weapon formed against me shall prosper. God is my protector."

2nd Mystery: The Flight into Egypt

> "Rise, take the child and his mother, and flee to Egypt. Stay there until I tell you, for Herod is going to search for the child to kill him." (Matthew 2:13)

Meditation: Mary and Joseph fled under divine instruction, becoming refugees. Even in exile, God's grace was at work, protecting their family.

Reflection: When life takes unexpected detours, can I trust that God's mercy is hidden in the disruption?

Affirmation: "I am guided. God's plans are unfolding, even when I don't understand."

3rd Mystery: The Rulers of Darkness

"The rulers thought they had done something powerful. But they merely fulfilled what was written." (Gospel of Philip, Logion 72 paraphrased)

Meditation: Oppressive leaders may seem invincible, but they ultimately serve a greater divine plan. God's justice transcends their cruelty.

Reflection: When faced with corrupt power, can I resist despair and walk in justice and truth?

Affirmation: "No system is greater than God. I rise in truth and light."

4th Mystery: Jesus Before Pilate

"My kingdom is not of this world. If it were, my servants would fight." (John 18:36)

Meditation: Jesus stood before earthly power with quiet dignity. His kingdom isn't defined by borders or governments but by love and justice.

Reflection: When I feel powerless, can I find strength in aligning with God's eternal kingdom?

Affirmation: "My peace comes from God, not the world. I serve a higher kingdom."

5th Mystery: The Triumph of the Lamb

"Then I saw a Lamb standing as though it had been slain, and with Him were the faithful." (Revelation 5:6)

Meditation: Even in death, the Lamb triumphed. Jesus' innocent sacrifice overcame the powers of this world with love, not violence.

Reflection: In times of suffering, can I trust that divine victory is achieved through endurance and love?

Affirmation: "I am aligned with the victorious Lamb. God's justice is on the way."

Closing Prayer

O Queen of Heaven, Bless all who live in fear today.

Stretch your hand over nations to shield the oppressed. Help us discern when to speak, when to stay, when to flee, and when to stand.

Pray for justice, courage, and peace. Mary, Undoer of Knots, untangle the chains of tyranny. Amen.

Peace Amid War, Genocide, and Violence

For those feeling the anguish of violent times

Opening Prayer

Heavenly Father, We come to You in the midst of a world torn by violence, war, and suffering.

Thank You for Your promise of peace that surpasses understanding. As we pray this Rosary for Peace, we ask for the intercession of: Our Lady Queen of Peace, to guide us in choosing compassion over conquest.

Our Lady of Sorrows, to join us in lament for the broken. Our Lady of Refuge, to shelter the displaced and grieving. Fill our hearts with hope and courage to be peacemakers in our time. Amen.

1st Mystery: The Slaughter of the Innocents

"Herod gave orders to kill all the boys in Bethlehem... and there was weeping and great mourning."(Matthew 2:16)

Meditation: War begins with fear and control, and ends in mourning. Mary's heart broke for the innocent then, as it breaks now.

Reflection: How do I respond to the suffering of innocents in the world?

Affirmation: "I do not turn away. I bear witness and pray for peace."

2nd Mystery: Jesus Weeps Over Jerusalem

> "As He approached Jerusalem and saw the city, He wept over it..." (Luke 19:41-42)

Meditation: Even Christ mourned the violence He foresaw. God does not delight in vengeance He weeps with the broken.

Reflection: Do I allow myself to lament with God?

Affirmation: "My grief is prayer. My tears have power."

3rd Mystery: Jesus Heals the Centurion's Servant

> "Truly I tell you, I have not found anyone in Israel with such great faith... and his servant was healed at that moment." (Matthew 8:8-10, 13)

Meditation: Even soldiers can act with compassion. Faith and humility can transform power into a force for healing.

Reflection: What power or privilege can I use to bring healing?

Affirmation: "My faith is stronger than fear. My actions can heal."

4th Mystery: The Passion of Christ

"He was pierced for our transgressions... and by His wounds we are healed." (Isaiah 53:5)

Meditation: Christ bore the full weight of human violence and transformed it into mercy. No atrocity is beyond His redemption.

Reflection: Where am I called to intercede for healing in the world?

Affirmation: "Christ bore all wounds. Love will have the final word."

5th Mystery: The Resurrected Christ Appears and Says, 'Peace Be With You'

"Jesus came and stood among them and said, 'Peace be with you." (John 20:19-21)

Meditation: Peace is not passive-it is presence. Christ enters our locked rooms, our fears, our traumas. His peace reaches every war zone of the soul.

Reflection: Where do I need to welcome Christ's peace today?

Affirmation: "Christ's peace is stronger than the violence of this world."

Closing Prayer

Our Lady, Queen of Peace, Hold this bleeding world in your arms.

Wrap the wounded, the displaced, and the grieving in your veil. Pray for the hearts of leaders, soldiers, and citizens - That compassion may triumph over conquest.

Teach us to choose mercy, to speak up, and to carry hope like a banner. Turn our weapons into tools of healing. Amen

Wisdom in the Age of AI and Tech Overload

For discernment in a world of rapid technological advancement, seeking God's wisdom above all else

Opening Prayer

Heavenly Father, We come before You in a world overwhelmed by technology, longing for clarity and wisdom. Thank You for the gift of innovation, but guide us to use it for good and not for harm. Grant us the humility to discern Your truth amidst the noise and distractions.

As we pray this Rosary for Wisdom, we ask for the intercession of:

- Our Lady Seat of Wisdom, to guide us toward holy understanding.

- Our Lady of Balance, to find balance amidst tech overload.

- Our Lady of Discernment, to choose what aligns with Your will.

May we anchor ourselves in Your truth, seeking wisdom not from screens but from Your eternal Word. Amen.

1st Mystery: The Tower of Babel - Humanity's Pride in Technology

> "'Let us make a name for ourselves...' But the Lord scattered them." (Genesis 11:4-9)

Meditation: When innovation becomes driven by ego, it divides us. True wisdom is rooted in reverence for God, not in human pride or ambition.

Reflection: Am I building my life on sacred truths or artificial importance?

Affirmation: "I seek wisdom, not vanity. I choose humility over control."

2nd Mystery: Jesus Retreats to the Desert

> "But Jesus often withdrew to lonely places and prayed." (Luke 5:16)

Meditation: Even Jesus, surrounded by crowds, stepped away into silence to connect with the Father. Solitude restores our souls and recenters us in God's presence.

Reflection: When was the last time I unplugged to simply be with God?

Affirmation: "I create space for silence. My soul needs stillness."

3rd Mystery: The Temptation in the Desert

"All these I will give you...' Jesus said, 'Away from me, Satan!'" (Matthew 4:8-10)

Meditation: The devil tempted Jesus with instant power. In the same way, technology can tempt us with ease, convenience, and control. Discernment is key to avoiding these traps.

Reflection: Am I allowing technology to shape my values or distract me from my calling?

Affirmation: "I am not ruled by machines. I am guided by the Spirit."

4th Mystery: The Voice of the Good Shepherd

"My sheep listen to my voice; I know them, and they follow me." (John 10:27)

Meditation: With so many voices competing for our attention, only God's voice brings clarity and life. His voice is quiet but unmistakably true.

Reflection: Whose voice am I tuning into the most each day?

Affirmation: "I hear God's voice above the noise."

5th Mystery: Paul's Warning on False Wisdom

"See to it that no one takes you captive through hollow and deceptive philosophy..."(Colossians 2:8)

Meditation: We are called to test what we're told and trust the Spirit over worldly knowledge. God's wisdom far surpasses human understanding or data-driven solutions.

Reflection: Do I seek divine understanding, or do I settle for human knowledge?

Affirmation: "I am wise in God. My soul is not for sale."

Closing Prayer

Guide us in this wired world to prioritize stillness over distraction.

When technology overwhelms and disconnects us from ourselves, lead us back to simplicity.

When artificial voices claim authority, help us hear the gentle whisper of God.

Anchor us in truth, in prayer, and in presence. Amen.

Internalized Racism and Division

For unity, dignity, and love beyond divisions of race, culture, or creed

Opening Prayer

O Blessed Mother, mirror of justice and vessel of unity, you who bore the Light of the world in your womb.

Teach us to love others as God loves beyond tribe, color, or creed.

Help us see ourselves as God sees us — beloved, dignified, divine. Heal every place in us where hatred, fear, or shame has made a home.

Intercede for a world where we honor our differences and celebrate the image of God in every soul. Amen.

1st Mystery: We Are All Made in God's Image

"So God created mankind in his own image... male and female he created them." (Genesis 1:27)

Meditation: Racism is a lie that contradicts the truth: every person reflects the Divine.

Reflection: Where have I believed or acted as if some people are more worthy than others?

Affirmation: "I am made in God's image. So is every person I meet."

2nd Mystery: The Good Samaritan

"Which of these was a neighbor...? The one who showed mercy." (Luke 10:36-37)

Meditation: The neighbor was not the one with the right religion or ethnicity - it was the one who loved.

Reflection: Am I judging others by their background or by their heart?

Affirmation: "I choose love over judgment, mercy over separation."

3rd Mystery: Jesus Welcomes the Outsider

"You are a Jew and I am a Samaritan woman. How can you ask me for a drink?" (John 4:9)

Meditation: Jesus shattered cultural and gender barriers to show divine dignity to a woman rejected by her people.

Reflection: Where have I excluded others - or myself - because of labels?

Affirmation: "I welcome others as Jesus welcomes me."

4th Mystery: "Whoever is Not Against Us is For Us"

> "Do not stop him... for whoever is not against us is for us." (Mark 9:38-40)

Meditation: Unity is not sameness—the Spirit moves where she wills.

Reflection: Can I honor the divine in other denominations or cultures, even if they're different from mine?

Affirmation: "I make room for the Spirit in all Her forms."

5th Mystery: Pentecost - All Nations, One Spirit

> "Each one heard them speaking in his own language." (Acts 2:6)

Meditation: The Spirit did not erase differences - She empowered every voice to be heard.

Reflection: Am I allowing space for diverse voices in my spiritual walk?

Affirmation: "I embrace unity without erasing identity."

Closing Prayer

Mother of Unity, Heal what has been divided by hate, ignorance, or pride.

Cleanse my heart of internalized lies and prejudices.

Make me a vessel of reconciliation in this fractured world.

Let your mantle of compassion stretch wide over every race, every culture, every creed. and may we all be one, as Christ prayed. Amen.

Climate Justice and Stewardship of Creation

For those who feel the grief of extinction, the dread of environmental collapse, and the yearning to heal and protect what God has made

Opening Prayer

Heavenly Father, Creator of all that is good, we come before You with hearts heavy with the grief of extinction and the fear of environmental collapse.

Yet, we are also filled with hope and a deep yearning to heal and protect the beautiful world You have entrusted to us.

As we pray this Rosary for Climate Justice and the Stewardship of Creation, we call upon the intercession of Our Lady Queen of Creation, Our Lady of Mount Carmel, and Our Lady of the Earth.

May their guidance inspire us to be faithful stewards of Your creation. Lord, remind us that "the earth is Yours, and everything in it" (Psalm 24:1), and help us to act with love, courage, and commitment to care for all that You have made. Amen.

1st Mystery: The Garden of Eden and Humanity's First Vocation

"The Lord God took the man and put him in the Garden of Eden to work it and take care of it." (Genesis 2:15)

Meditation: Before sin, there was stewardship. Humanity's first divine role was to care for the earth. This sacred calling still stands.

Reflection: Am I honoring my role as a caretaker of creation?

Affirmation: "I am called to nurture, not consume."

2nd Mystery: Noah and the Ark - God's Covenant with All Life

"This is the sign of the covenant... between me and every living creature... I have set my rainbow in the clouds." (Genesis 9:12-13)

Meditation: God's covenant isn't just with humans - it's with all living things. We are part of an interconnected web of life, bound by divine promise.

Reflection: Do I live in a way that honors all creatures and future generations?

Affirmation: "God's covenant includes the earth - and I will honor it."

3rd Mystery: Jesus Calms the Storm

"He got up, rebuked the wind... 'Quiet! Be still!' The wind died down and it was completely calm." (Mark 4:39-40)

Meditation: Even nature responds to Christ. In times of chaos, Jesus brings peace and power to still the storm.

Reflection: How can I turn my eco-anxiety into prayerful trust and action?

Affirmation: "Even in climate chaos, Christ is in the boat with me."

4th Mystery: The Transfiguration - A Glimpse of Glory in Nature

"His face shone like the sun, and His clothes became white as light." (Matthew 17:2)

Meditation: Divine light shines through creation. Mountains become altars; clouds become witnesses. Nature reveals God's glory.

Reflection: Do I let myself be awed by the beauty of creation?

Affirmation: "Creation reveals the glory of God. I will protect that glory."

5th Mystery: The New Heaven and New Earth

"Then I saw a new heaven and a new earth... 'Behold, I make all things new.'" (Revelation 21:1-5)

Meditation: God's plan ends not in destruction, but in restoration. Renewal is the ultimate hope for all creation.

Reflection: How can I live as a co-creator of a restored world?

Affirmation: "I partner with God in restoring what is broken."

Closing Prayer

Our Lady, Queen of All Creation, You who carried the Lord of Life in your womb, Teach us to cherish all life - not just human, but winged and rooted, wild and flowing.

Intercede for this groaning earth. Forgive our carelessness, awaken our reverence.

Show us how to live simply, love deeply, and protect fiercely.

May we become gardeners of justice and prophets of renewal.

Amen.

Freedom from Debt

For those seeking financial freedom and transformation

Opening Prayer

O dearest Mother Mary, Our Lady of Good Remedy and Our Lady of Perpetual Help, I come before you with a heart heavy with financial burdens and debt. Just as you interceded for the saints and suffering throughout history, intercede for me now.

Ask your Son, Jesus, who multiplied loaves, paid the temple tax with a coin from a fish, and canceled our spiritual debt, to grant me wisdom, discipline, opportunity, and provision.

I pray this rosary not just for material freedom, but for the transformation of my heart, habits, and hope.

Amen.

1st Mystery: God Sees and Provides

"So Abraham called that place 'The Lord Will Provide.' And to this day it is said, 'On the mountain of the Lord it will be provided.'" (Genesis 22:14)

Meditation: Even when Isaac was bound and the situation seemed hopeless, God had already prepared the ram. He sees your sacrifice and has a remedy in place.

Reflection: Where in your life can you begin to trust that God already has provision waiting for you?

Affirmation: "God is already providing a way out for me. I will see His remedy."

2nd Mystery: The Widow's Oil Multiplied

> "Go, sell the oil and pay your debts. You and your sons can live on what is left." (2 Kings 4:1-7)

Meditation: The miracle began with a small act of faith. The oil flowed as the widow acted in obedience. What seems small in your hands can overflow in God's.

Reflection: What simple act of faith can you do today to invite God's multiplication into your finances?

Affirmation: "God multiplies what I offer in faith. My small becomes abundance."

3rd Mystery: Jesus Cancels the Debt

> "Having canceled the charge of our legal indebtedness... He has taken it away, nailing it to the cross." (Colossians 2:14)

Meditation: Jesus understands debt-not His own, but ours. He paid what we could not, spiritually and symbolically. That same mercy can renew your finances.

Reflection: How can receiving Jesus' mercy help you release shame and take positive financial steps?

Affirmation: "Jesus paid my greatest debt. I walk forward in freedom."

4th Mystery: Joseph's Strategy in Egypt

> "Joseph collected all the food produced... and stored it in the cities... It was so much that he stopped keeping records because it was beyond measure." (Genesis 41:48-49)

Meditation: Joseph didn't just receive revelation-he planned, stored, and acted. Ask the Holy Spirit for practical wisdom. You too can build overflow.

Reflection: What financial habits do you need to develop to store wisely and prepare for the future?

Affirmation: "God gives me strategy, not just survival. I will prosper with wisdom."

5th Mystery: The Good Steward

"Whoever can be trusted with very little can also be trusted with much." (Luke 16:10)

Meditation: Debt does not define your destiny. As you manage what you have with faithfulness, the door to increase opens.

Reflection: How can you be faithful with what you have today, no matter how small?

Affirmation: "I am becoming a faithful steward. Little by little, I am free."

Closing Prayer

Dearest Mother Mary, Our Lady of Good Remedy, you were given by the Church as a source of miraculous help in times of need. And you, Our Lady of Perpetual Help, never cease interceding for your children. I entrust to you my desire for financial freedom.

Take my fear, shame, and anxiety and transform them into action, wisdom, and trust.

Intercede for divine solutions, open doors, and provision from unexpected places.

Help me walk with your Son in wisdom and purpose, and lead me out of this wilderness into abundance.

Amen.

Struggling with Immigration and Refugee Journeys

For those facing the challenges of displacement, searching for refuge, and seeking hope in the face of adversity

Opening Prayer

Our Lady of Migrants, we come before you with broken yet hopeful hearts as we pray this Rosary for those struggling with the hardships of immigration and seeking refuge.

Your Son, Jesus Christ, knew the trials of being displaced, fleeing danger, and trusting in God's providence.

We ask for your loving intercession, as you walked alongside Jesus on His own journeys, to guide and console all those who are exiled and displaced. May these prayers bring comfort, courage, and hope to those searching for safety and the promise of a better future.

Amen.

1st Mystery: The Flight into Egypt

"When they had gone, an angel of the Lord appeared to Joseph in a dream. 'Get up,' he said, 'take the child and His mother and escape to Egypt. Stay there until I tell you, for Herod is going to search for the child to kill him.'" (Matthew 2:13-14)

Meditation: The Holy Family faced the fear and uncertainty of fleeing their homeland to escape danger, trusting in God's plan to protect them. Refugees and immigrants today often make similar sacrifices, seeking safety and a better life for their loved ones.

Reflection: Do I seek to extend compassion and support to those forced to leave their homes behind?

Affirmation: "I open my heart to welcome and care for those fleeing hardship, trusting in God's mercy."

2nd Mystery: The Exile of the Israelites

"The Israelites said to them, 'If only we had died by the Lord's hand in Egypt! There we sat around pots of meat and ate all the food we wanted, but you have brought us out into this desert to starve...' Then the Lord said to Moses, 'I will rain down bread from heaven for you." (Exodus 16:3-4)

Meditation: The pain of exile is often accompanied by moments of doubt and despair. Yet God provided for His people in the wilderness, offering them manna from heaven and the promise of a brighter tomorrow.

Reflection: How can I be a source of encouragement and provision to others in moments of desperation and need?

Affirmation: "I share God's love with those in exile, offering hope and support wherever I can."

3rd Mystery: Ruth and Naomi's Journey

"Where you go I will go, and where you stay I will stay. Your people will be my people and your God my God." (Ruth 1:16-17)

Meditation: Ruth's boundless loyalty to Naomi and willingness to leave behind her homeland to walk an unfamiliar path speaks to the trust and love that transform sorrow into hope on a difficult journey.

Reflection: Do I strive to emulate Ruth's spirit of loyalty and love as I support others on their life's path?

Affirmation: "I remain steadfast in offering love, friendship, and solidarity to those in need."

4th Mystery: The Return from Exile in Babylon

"Any of His people among you may go up to Jerusalem in Judah and build the temple of the Lord, the God of Israel, the God who is in Jerusalem, and may their God be with them." (Ezra 1:3)

Meditation: The return of the Israelites to their homeland demonstrates the power of restoration and renewal after trials of exile. God's faithfulness sustains those who persevered through suffering.

Reflection: Do I trust in God's promise to restore and renew even in the most challenging times?

Affirmation: "I hold fast to God's promise of restoration and work to strengthen those seeking peace."

5th Mystery: Jesus' Ministry to the Outcast

"The Spirit of the Lord is on me, because He has anointed me to proclaim good news to the poor. He has sent me to proclaim freedom for the prisoners and recovery of sight for the blind, to set the oppressed free." (Luke 4:18)

Meditation: Jesus' mission was to care for the marginalized and bring hope to the oppressed. Immigrants and refugees, often overlooked or misunderstood, are beloved in the eyes of God.

Reflection: How can I follow Jesus' example by being an advocate for justice and a source of comfort to the displaced?

Affirmation: "I honor Jesus' mission of uplifting the marginalized and stand in solidarity with all who seek refuge."

Closing Prayer

> Blessed Mother, you who fled to Egypt with the infant Jesus,
>
> Pray for all those enduring the hardships of immigration, exile, and displacement.
>
> Guide them to places of safety, strengthen them with hope, and fill them with trust in God's providence.
>
> May we, too, answer God's call to be beacons of care, compassion, and mercy in our world.
>
> Through your intercession, may those who struggle find solace, rest, and restoration in the Lord's loving arms.
>
> Amen.

10

Rosaries for Overcoming Addictions and Behaviors

For freedom Christ has set us free; stand firm therefore, and do not submit again to a yoke of slavery." - Galatians 5:1

Addictions and negative behaviors can feel like insurmountable chains that hold us back from living the full and abundant life God desires for us. Whether the struggle lies in substance abuse, pornography, or even patterns of negativity like indulgence in harmful entertainment or gossip, these battles can weigh heavily on our hearts and minds. The grip of these behaviors can lead to feelings of shame, isolation, and hopelessness, overshadowing the joy and peace we are called to experience.

Breaking free from these cycles requires strength, perseverance, and most importantly, trust in God's transforming grace. By turning to prayer and reflection, we can invite God into the darkest corners of our struggles, allowing His love and mercy to carry us through the path of healing and renewal. Praying the rosary is a powerful way to seek these graces, as it helps us draw closer to Mary, our spiritual mother, who intercedes for us with her boundless love. Through the rosary, we receive graces from Mary that strengthen our will, guide us towards virtue, and remind us that we are never alone in our battles.

The following rosaries are designed to support you in overcoming these challenges. By meditating on their mysteries, you can find hope, courage, and the spiritual strength to break free from the chains of addiction and negative habits, while embracing the graces Mary offers to align your life more closely with God's will and His infinite love for you.

Pornography Addiction

For those seeking liberation from addiction and a path of healing and dignity

Opening Prayer

> Heavenly Father, we come before You with hearts burdened by the weight of addiction.
>
> You are the source of all healing and freedom, and we long to be restored.
>
> As we pray this Rosary for Freedom from Pornography, we ask for the intercession of Our Lady of Perpetual Help, Our Lady of Mercy, and Our Lady of Sorrows to guide us.
>
> Grant us the grace to see ourselves as You do with love, dignity, and hope.
>
> Amen.

1st Mystery: The Fall of David and Bathsheba

"From the roof he saw a woman bathing. The woman was very beautiful, and David sent someone to find out about her..." (2 Samuel 11:2-4)

Meditation: David's lust clouded his judgment, leading him to objectify and sin further. Addiction often begins with a glance, spiraling into deeper harm.

Reflection: Where have I turned others into objects? What is my heart truly seeking?

Affirmation: "I am made for love, not fantasy. My eyes can be healed."

2nd Mystery: Jesus and the Woman Caught in Adultery

"Jesus said, 'Neither do I condemn you. Go, and sin no more." (John 8:10-11)

Meditation: Jesus didn't shame the woman - He freed her. His mercy is greater than any sin. We are seen and loved, not defined by our past.

Reflection: Can I receive mercy today, even when I feel ashamed?

Affirmation: "I am not condemned. I am loved into freedom."

3rd Mystery: Job Makes a Covenant with His Eyes

> "I made a covenant with my eyes not to look lustfully at a young woman." (Job 31:1)

Meditation: Job didn't suppress his desires — he redirected them with a holy vow. Healing starts with reclaiming our gaze and aligning it with honor.

Reflection: What covenant can I make with my body, mind, and eyes today?

Affirmation: "My body and eyes belong to God. I choose sacred vision."

4th Mystery: Jesus Heals the Possessed Man

> "They saw the man who had been possessed... sitting there, dressed and in his right mind." (Mark 5:15)

Meditation: This man was chained, isolated, and consumed - much like those trapped in addiction. Jesus restored him fully, showing that freedom is always possible.

Reflection: What chains do I need Jesus to break today?

Affirmation: "I am not my addiction. I am already being restored."

5th Mystery: The Pure in Heart Will See God

"Blessed are the pure in heart, for they shall see God." (Matthew 5:8)

Meditation: Purity is not about shame - it's about clarity, peace, and presence. Freedom allows us to see others, ourselves, and God rightly.

Reflection: What vision of myself and others needs to be restored?

Affirmation: "I see with love. I live in truth. I am enough."

Closing Prayer

Our Lady of Perpetual Help, You who never turn away the broken,

Wrap your mantle around me as I struggle and rise again.

Let me not be defined by failure, but transformed by grace.

Help me desire intimacy over escape, truth over fantasy, and freedom that is rooted in love.

Amen.

Drug Addiction

For those seeking liberation from dependency and a path of healing and grace

Opening Prayer

Heavenly Father, we come to You with hearts burdened by the weight of addiction.

You are the source of all freedom and healing, and we long for liberation. Guide us as we pray this Rosary for Freedom from Drug Addiction.

We ask for the intercession of :

- Our Lady of Mercy
- Our Lady of Recovery
- and Our Lady of Lourdes

to walk with us on this journey.

Grant us the strength to surrender, the courage to heal, and the grace to rediscover life in Your love.

Amen.

1st Mystery: The Israelites Long for Egypt Again

> "We remember the fish we ate in Egypt at no cost... but now we have lost our appetite; we never see anything but this manna!" (Numbers 11:4-6)

Meditation: The familiar pain can feel safer than the unknown healing. Like Israel craving slavery over freedom, addiction can deceive us into believing that bondage brings comfort.

Reflection: Where have I mistaken captivity for comfort?

Affirmation: "I was made for freedom, not for chains."

2nd Mystery: Jesus Heals the Man at the Pool

> "Jesus asked him, 'Do you want to be made well?'... At once the man was cured." (John 5:6-9)

Meditation: Healing begins with desire. Jesus didn't assume the man's answer-He asked. This mystery reminds us of the power of wanting wellness, even when the journey feels difficult.

Reflection: Do I believe healing is possible for me?

Affirmation: "I want to be well- and I will rise."

3rd Mystery: The Prodigal Son Returns

> "When he came to his senses... he got up and went to his father. But while he was still a long way off, his father ran to him." (Luke 15:17-20)

Meditation: No matter how far we've strayed, there is always a way back. The Father meets us with open arms, offering love without shame, only grace.

Reflection: What keeps me from coming home to love?

Affirmation: "I am never too far gone for grace."

4th Mystery: Mary at the Wedding of Cana

> "They have no wine... Do whatever He tells you." (John 2:3-5)

Meditation: Mary notices the need and brings it to Jesus. She doesn't judge the lack but trusts in His ability to provide. In our emptiness, she intercedes for us, leading us to grace.

Reflection: What emptiness am I afraid to bring to God?

Affirmation: "My needs are not shameful. I am open to grace."

5th Mystery: Jesus in the Garden of Gethsemane

"My soul is overwhelmed with sorrow... yet not my will, but Yours be done." (Matthew 26:38-39)

Meditation: The hardest battles are often fought in the quiet of the garden, before the cross. Jesus faced His agony and surrendered to the Father's will. Recovery also requires daily surrender, one moment at a time.

Reflection: What part of me needs to surrender today?

Affirmation: "I can face the pain. I am not alone in the garden."

Closing Prayer

Our Lady of Mercy,

Mother who watches over us in our struggles, hold us as we take this difficult journey toward freedom.

Intercede when we are too weary to pray, strengthen us when we feel weak,

And pour healing grace over every wound.

May our lives become a testimony to the power of Your love, that freedom is possible, healing is real, and grace never abandons us.

Amen.

Disordered Eating

For balance, gratitude, and peace with food and body

Opening Prayer

> Beloved Mother,
>
> We ask for your help in healing our relationship with food and our bodies.
>
> May we neither idolize nor despise nourishment, but receive it with gratitude.
>
> Teach us the holiness of balance and the power of fasting rightly ordered.
>
> Amen.

1st Mystery: Jesus' Forty Days - Victory Over Fleshly Temptation

> "Man shall not live by bread alone, but by every word that comes from the mouth of God." (Matthew 4:4)

Meditation: Jesus teaches us to rely on the Spirit, not impulsive cravings. Food is not a god-God is our true source.

Reflection: Can I separate my identity from what I eat and find my worth in God alone?

Affirmation: "Food does not control me. I am nourished by God's Word."

2nd Mystery: Daniel's Fast - Setting Apart Our Bodies

"He resolved not to defile himself with the royal food and wine." (Daniel 1:8)

Meditation: Daniel reminds us that some foods-and attitudes-defile. Sacred discipline can honor both body and soul.

Reflection: How can I honor God by making intentional choices about how I care for my body?

Affirmation: "I choose what honors God. I care for my body with intention."

3rd Mystery: The Feeding of the Five Thousand - God Provides Enough

"They all ate and were satisfied." (Matthew 14:20)

Meditation: Jesus doesn't just meet needs-He satisfies. Disordered eating stems from fear of lack. But in Christ, there is abundance.

Reflection: Do I trust that God will provide what I need, without fear of scarcity?

Affirmation: "God satisfies me fully. I no longer fear emptiness."

4th Mystery: Fasting and Deliverance - Power Through Surrender

> "This kind does not go out except by prayer and fasting." (Matthew 17:21)

Meditation: Fasting is not punishment-it's empowerment. Done rightly, it breaks bondage and invites spiritual clarity.

Reflection: Am I open to fasting as a way to grow closer to God?

Affirmation: "Fasting strengthens me. I fast not to shrink, but to grow."

5th Mystery: Jesus Breaks Bread - Communion Over Control

> "He took bread, gave thanks and broke it." (Luke 22:19)

Meditation: Food becomes holy in Jesus' hands. In Him, eating is sacred-not sinful, not shameful, not stressful.

Reflection: Can I approach food with gratitude and peace, rather than control or fear?

Affirmation: "I eat with peace. My body is a temple, not a battleground."

Closing Prayer

> Mother Mary, you nursed Christ with love.
>
> Help us reclaim our relationship with food as one of dignity, gratitude, and sacred rhythm.
>
> Guard us against shame and gluttony. Restore our joy in the table of the Lord.
>
> Amen.

TV Addiction

For those seeking to break free from the distractions of reality TV and embrace a life of peace, presence, and connection

Opening Prayer

Heavenly Father,

We come before You longing for freedom from the noise and distractions that pull us away from Your peace.

Reality TV often tempts us with drama, comparison, and escape, but we desire to live fully in the beauty of real life. Through this Rosary, we seek Your guidance to refocus our hearts and minds on what truly matters.

We ask for the intercession of Our Lady of Peace, Our Lady of Discernment, and Our Lady of Solitude to help us embrace stillness, truth, and the richness of Your presence.

Amen.

1st Mystery: Lot's Wife Looks Back

"But Lot's wife looked back, and she became a pillar of salt." (Genesis 19:26)

Meditation: Lot's wife looked back toward destruction, unable to let go of the drama and chaos of her past. Reality TV tempts us to do the same, consuming chaos instead of walking forward. True healing invites us to turn away from distractions and move toward peace.

Reflection: What am I looking back at that's keeping me stuck?

Affirmation: "I turn toward peace, not drama."

2nd Mystery: Martha Is Distracted by Many Things

> "Martha was distracted... but Mary has chosen what is better." (Luke 10:40-42)

Meditation: Distraction isn't inherently bad, but it keeps us from focusing on what truly feeds the soul. Like Martha, we are called to let go of constant stimulation and return to the Presence that sustains us.

Reflection: What stillness am I avoiding by staying distracted?

Affirmation: "I choose what feeds my soul."

3rd Mystery: Guard Your Heart

> "Above all else, guard your heart, for everything you do flows from it." (Proverbs 4:23)

Meditation: Our eyes and ears are gateways to the heart. Reality TV often fills us with noise, conflict, and envy, but our hearts are too sacred for such clutter. Choose to protect your peace and let in only what helps you grow.

Reflection: Is what I'm watching helping me grow or shrinking my spirit?

Affirmation: "I protect my peace and guard my heart."

4th Mystery: Jesus in the Desert

> "The devil showed Him all the kingdoms of the world... 'All this I will give you,' he said, 'if you will bow down and worship me.'" (Matthew 4:8-10)

Meditation: The enemy often tempts us with spectacle and power but at a cost. Reality TV can become an altar where we idolize fame, wealth, and control. Jesus chose truth and simplicity over empty promises.

Reflection: Where am I being tempted by fantasy instead of truth?

Affirmation: "I do not need a show. I live in reality with God."

5th Mystery: The Transfiguration of Christ

> "He was transfigured before them... His face shone like the sun."(Matthew 17:2)

Meditation: True beauty is found in divine radiance, not edited highlight reels. Reality TV masks people in roles, while God reveals us as we are, transforming us into light.

Reflection: What would it feel like to stop watching and start shining?

Affirmation: "I choose my life over someone else's show."

Closing Prayer

> Our Lady of Peace, free me from the need for noise, from the thirst for gossip and glamour.
>
> Teach me to rest in what is real, To find joy in unedited moments.
>
> Fill the empty space where entertainment ruled with the presence of God and the richness of stillness.
>
> Let me live fully-awake, aware, and whole.
>
> Amen.

Jealousy

For those wanting freedom from envy

Opening Prayer

Mother Mary, gentle heart and mirror of humility, intercede for us as we bring before God our wounds of comparison and envy.

Cleanse our hearts of resentment and renew in us the truth that we are uniquely loved.

Help us walk the path of contentment, admiration, and gratitude.

Amen.

1st Mystery: Cain and Abel - The Wound of Comparison

"Then the Lord said to Cain, 'Why are you angry? Why is your face downcast? If you do what is right, will you not be accepted?'" (Genesis 4:6-7)

Meditation: Like Cain, we often turn envy into anger and division. But God reminds us: righteousness and trust bring acceptance, not rivalry.

Reflection: When I feel tempted to compare myself with others, can I rest in God's unique love for me?

Affirmation: "I am uniquely loved. I have a place at the altar of grace."

2nd Mystery: Joseph's Brothers - Jealousy Destroys Unity

> "They saw that their father loved him more... so they hated him and could not speak a kind word to him." (Genesis 37:4)

Meditation: Jealousy blinds us to the humanity of others. Yet even in betrayal, God can bring restoration—as He did through Joseph.

Reflection: How can I release envy and choose to celebrate others instead of resenting them?

Affirmation: "I release envy and choose peace. God's plan for me is good."

3rd Mystery: Saul and David - Insecurity vs. Anointing

> "Saul was very angry... They have ascribed to David ten thousands... What more can he have but the kingdom?" (1 Samuel 18:8)

Meditation: When we define ourselves by others' victories, we live in fear. Let us rest in God's calling without competition.

Reflection: Can I trust in my own anointing, even when others succeed?

Affirmation: "Another's success is not my failure. I trust in my own anointing."

4th Mystery: The Workers in the Vineyard - Divine Fairness

> "Are you envious because I am generous?" (Matthew 20:15)

Meditation: God's grace is not a transaction-it is a gift. Envy vanishes when we understand that His love is abundant.

Reflection: Can I embrace the truth that God's generosity is enough for everyone?

Affirmation: "I celebrate the goodness others receive. God's generosity is not scarce."

5th Mystery: Peter and John - Staying in Our Lane

> "Peter asked, 'Lord, what about him?' Jesus answered, 'What is that to you? You must follow me.'"(John 21:21-22)

Meditation: Jesus calls us to walk our own road. When we stop looking side to side, we find the strength to move forward.

Reflection: Am I focused on my calling, or am I distracted by comparison?

Affirmation: "I follow Christ, not comparison. My calling is enough."

Closing Prayer

Holy Mary, you rejoiced even when others were lifted up- pray that we may walk free from the heavy chains of envy.

Teach us to love purely, admire freely, and bless openly.

Amen.

Gossip

For those seeking to purify their speech, release harmful talk, and embrace words that heal and bless

Opening Prayer

We seek freedom from gossip and harmful words. Gossip wounds both the speaker and the listener, pulling us away from truth and love.

Through this Rosary, guide us to transform our speech, align our hearts with Your will, and use our words to bring healing and unity.

We ask for the intercession of Our Lady of Silence, Our Lady of Good Counsel, and Our Lady of Mount Carmel to help us guard our tongues and speak only in love.

Amen.

1st Mystery: Miriam Speaks Against Moses

"Miriam and Aaron began to speak against Moses... the Lord's anger burned... and Miriam became leprous."(Numbers 12:1-2, 10)

Meditation: Even spiritual leaders fall into gossip. Miriam's jealousy led to words that divided and wounded. God shows us that gossip is not harmless - it can spiritually infect us and sow division.

Reflection: Where does gossip mask jealousy or comparison in my life?

Affirmation: "My words carry power. I choose to speak life."

2nd Mystery: Jesus Is Silent Before Pilate

> "But when He was accused... He gave no answer... Jesus made no reply, not even to a single charge."(Matthew 27:12-14)

Meditation: Even when slandered, Jesus chose silence. Not every accusation or opinion needs a response. Sometimes, silence is the most powerful witness.

Reflection: When can I hold silence instead of fueling harm?

Affirmation: "I do not need to speak to be strong."

3rd Mystery: James on the Power of the Tongue

> "The tongue is a small part of the body... but it can set the whole course of one's life on fire." (James 3:5-6)

Meditation: James reminds us that the tongue can bless or destroy. Gossip may seem small, but its impact can spread like wildfire, leaving lasting harm.

Reflection: How have I underestimated the effect of my words?

Affirmation: "My speech is sacred. I release harmful talk."

4th Mystery: The Pharisee and the Tax Collector

> "The Pharisee stood and prayed: 'God, I thank you that I am not like other people...'" (Luke 18:11-14)

Meditation: Gossip often disguises pride. Instead of naming our pain or insecurities, we compare and judge others. Jesus exalts humility over judgment or self-righteousness.

Reflection: Where does gossip try to make me feel more valuable?

Affirmation: "I release judgment and choose grace."

5th Mystery: Mary Treasured Things in Her Heart

> "But Mary treasured up all these things and pondered them in her heart." (Luke 2:19)

Meditation: Mary didn't spread news or react impulsively - she pondered and sought wisdom. Her quiet strength invites us to consider the sacredness of silence and intentional speech.

Reflection: Can I let silence become a sacred part of my speech?

Affirmation: "I speak less, and love more deeply."

Closing Prayer

> Our Lady of Silence,
>
> Teach me to guard my tongue, that my words may bless, not bruise.
>
> Free me from the habit of gossip, from the rush of judgment, and the thrill of tearing others down.
>
> Replace chatter with charity, and loose my tongue only in love.
>
> Amen.

Social Media Addiction

For those seeking freedom from social media's grip and a return to peace, presence, and connection

Opening Prayer

Heavenly Father, we come to You seeking healing from the distractions, comparisons, and restlessness caused by social media addiction.

You call us to a life of presence, peace, and freedom.

As we pray this Rosary, we ask for the intercession of Our Lady of Quiet Light to guide us back to simplicity, wholeness, and a deeper connection with You.

Amen.

1st Mystery: Eve Sees the Forbidden Fruit

"The woman saw that the tree was good for food... and desirable for gaining wisdom, so she took and ate." (Genesis 3:6)

Meditation: The first temptation came through the eyes. It appeared good and promised wisdom, but it brought disconnection. Social media often mirrors this enticing and promising fulfillment, yet leaving us empty and craving more.

Reflection: What am I trying to feel or prove when I reach for my phone?

Affirmation: "I do not need to consume to feel complete. I rest in enoughness."

2nd Mystery: Elijah Hears God in the Whisper

"The Lord was not in the wind... nor the earthquake... nor the fire, but in a still, small voice." (1 Kings 19:11-12)

Meditation: God's presence is not found in noise or spectacle but in quiet stillness. Scrolling numbs us with endless noise, while healing comes when we create space to truly listen.

Reflection: Where can I choose silence over stimulation today?

Affirmation: "I make room for peace. I choose the whisper."

3rd Mystery: The Pharisee and the Tax Collector

"The Pharisee stood and prayed... 'Thank God I'm not like other people.' But the tax collector beat his breast..."(Luke 18:11-14)

Meditation: Comparison destroys connection. Social media encourages judgment, envy, and performance, but God values humility and honesty over the highlight reel.

Reflection: Who am I comparing myself to and what truth does that cover up?

Affirmation: "I am already worthy. I release comparison."

4th Mystery: Jesus Withdraws to Lonely Places

"But Jesus often withdrew to lonely places and prayed."(Luke 5:16)

Meditation: Even Jesus needed time away from the crowds. Solitude wasn't loneliness, it was sacred renewal. We don't need to stay "on" all the time to be loved or valued.

Reflection: What would it feel like to unplug - even for a little while?

Affirmation: "Silence is not absence. It is healing."

5th Mystery: Mary Ponders in Her Heart

"But Mary treasured up all these things and pondered them in her heart." (Luke 2:19)

Meditation: Mary didn't share, post, or explain - she pondered. Healing from social media addiction begins with reclaiming the sacredness of our inner world. Not everything holy needs to be shared.

Reflection: What sacred moment can I keep just for me and God?

Affirmation: "I hold holy space within. I do not need an audience."

Closing Prayer

Mother Mary, you who lived simply and fully, teach me to unplug from what numbs and distracts.

Heal the craving for approval, the fatigue of comparison, and the noise that drowns out my spirit.

Lead me into quiet, presence, and grace. help me rest in who I already am-loved, chosen, and enough.

Amen.

Releasing Control

For surrendering, softening, and trusting in divine timing

Opening Prayer

Mother Mary,

You who surrendered with grace and strength, calm my need to control, fix, and perfect.

Let me rest in the hands of the God who carries worlds. Let me live the prayer: "Let it be done."

Amen.

1st Mystery: Martha is Distracted by Many Things

"Martha, Martha... you are worried and upset about many things, but only one thing is necessary."(Luke 10:41-42)

Meditation: Martha, in her busyness, missed the peace available in Jesus' presence. He gently reminded her that love doesn't need to be earned.

Reflection: Where am I doing too much out of fear I'm not enough?

Affirmation: "I release the need to earn love. I choose presence over perfection."

2nd Mystery: Abraham Surrenders Isaac

> "Do not lay a hand on the boy... now I know that you fear God, because you have not withheld your son."(Genesis 22:9-12)

Meditation: Abraham trusted God completely, releasing his most precious gift. His surrender allowed for transformation, not loss.

Reflection: What am I afraid to surrender - and what might God do with it if I did?

Affirmation: "I trust what I release will be transformed, not lost."

3rd Mystery: Jesus Calms the Storm

> "'Peace! Be still!' Then the wind died down... He said, 'Why are you so afraid?'"(Mark 4:39-40)

Meditation: Instead of controlling the storm, Jesus trusted and commanded stillness. Calm, not effort, brought the miracle.

Reflection: What part of my life do I need to stop managing and start entrusting?

Affirmation: "The storm is not mine to fix. I choose calm over control."

4th Mystery: The Prodigal Son's Father Lets Him Go

"While he was still a long way off, his father saw him and was filled with compassion."(Luke 15:11-24)

Meditation: The father didn't chase or shame his son. Instead, he released him in love, trusting he would return freely.

Reflection: Who or what do I need to lovingly release?

Affirmation: "Letting go is not weakness - it is love and wisdom."

5th Mystery: Mary's Fiat - Let It Be Done

"I am the handmaid of the Lord. Let it be done to me according to your word."(Luke 1:38)

Meditation: Mary's surrender wasn't passive - it was powerful. By releasing her future, she made way for divine transformation.

Reflection: Where am I being invited to say "yes" - even if I don't have control?

Affirmation: "Let it be done in me. I release the outcome."

Closing Prayer

Mother Mary,

Teach me to release control and trust in God's timing.

May I let go of what was never mine to hold and rest in divine hands.

Let me walk in surrender, knowing all is carried by the One who commands the stars.

Amen.

Low Self Esteem

For uprooting lies, breaking shame, and reclaiming divine self-worth

Opening Prayer

> Mother Mary,
>
> You who see with heaven's eyes, wrap me in your mantle.
>
> Teach me to bless my softness, my strength, my becoming, my brokenness, my beauty.
>
> Let me remember: I am worthy — not because I am perfect, but because I am divinely loved.
>
> Amen.

1st Mystery: You Are Made in God's Image

> "So God created man in his own image... male and female he created them."(Genesis 1:27)

Meditation: You were not an accident. Your body, your personality, your soul - all handcrafted by Divine Love. Every time you hate yourself, you forget who sculpted you.

Reflection: Where have I forgotten that I was made in God's image?

Affirmation: "I am made in the image of beauty, purpose, and love."

2nd Mystery: The Lord Looks at the Heart

> "People look at the outward appearance, but the Lord looks at the heart." (1 Samuel 16:7)

Meditation: The world may judge how you look, what you wear, or what you've achieved. But God sees your heart - the eternal part of you. And He calls it good.

Reflection: What would shift if I saw myself the way God sees me?

Affirmation: "My worth is not defined by appearance or status."

3rd Mystery: Jesus Sees the Woman at the Well

> "He told me everything I ever did... and still offered me living water." (John 4:17-18, 28-29)

Meditation: She was shamed and isolated, but Jesus spoke to her with love and called her worthy of eternal love. He saw her, all of her, and did not reject her.

Reflection: What parts of myself do I hide out of shame and can I bring them into the light?

Affirmation: "I am fully seen and still deeply loved."

4th Mystery: You Are God's Masterpiece

"For we are God's masterpiece, created in Christ Jesus for good works." (Ephesians 2:10)

Meditation: You are not broken. You are becoming. A masterpiece in progress - not because of perfection, but because of the hands that hold you.

Reflection: What "flaw" do I need to stop cursing and start blessing?

Affirmation: "I am a masterpiece in the making. I honor who I am becoming."

5th Mystery: Mary Sings Her Worth in the Magnificat

"The Almighty has done great things for me... and holy is his name." (Luke 1:46-49)

Meditation: Mary didn't shrink. She magnified. She saw herself as chosen, blessed, and favored not because of ego, but because she knew who loved her.

Reflection: What divine greatness has been done in me that I'm afraid to claim?

Affirmation: "I magnify my worth. I will not shrink to be loved."

Closing Prayer

Mother Mary,

Let me see myself through heaven's eyes.

Teach me to uproot lies, break shame, and plant seeds of divine self-worth.

I am worthy not because of what I've done, but because I am loved.

Amen.

11

Rosaries for Work, Career and Calling

"Commit your work to the Lord, and your plans will be established." - Proverbs 16:3

Work touches every part of life-our identity, our dignity, our time, and our trust. Whether you're searching for a new job, praying for provision, trying to leave a toxic workplace, or discerning your true vocation, these rosaries invite you to bring your labor into the light of God's presence.

The world often defines us by what we do - but Heaven sees deeper. These prayers will guide you not just to ask for doors to open, but to seek work that aligns with your soul, your family, and your purpose.

Each mystery is crafted for specific moments in your work life:

- When you feel stuck
- When you feel unseen
- When you're daring to dream

- When you're weighed down with responsibility

- When you're ready to build something new

Let these rosaries be your ladder of peace. Your quiet meeting room with the Divine.

Career Discernment and Clarity

For those wondering about work opportunities

Opening Prayer

Our Lady, Seat of Wisdom, hear my plea,

In life's confusion, stay near to me.

Through daily noise and paths unclear, help me find peace, and draw You near.

Quiet my heart, let God's voice be known, guide me with courage, I'm not alone.

With trust in His timing, I'll follow the way, walk with me, Mother, both night and day.

Amen

1st Mystery - Samuel's Call

"Speak, Lord, for your servant is listening."(1 Samuel 3:10)

Meditation: Like Samuel, we must quiet ourselves to hear God's direction. Discernment begins with deep listening.

Reflection: Am I truly open to what God may be saying - even if it's not what I expected?

Affirmation: "I trust God to guide my steps."

2nd Mystery - Trust in the Lord

"Trust in the Lord with all your heart... and He will make straight your paths."(Proverbs 3:5-6)

Meditation: When logic and options become overwhelming, surrender is the path to peace.

Reflection: Where am I relying too much on my own understanding instead of divine wisdom?

Affirmation: "God is directing my path with care."

3rd Mystery - The Call of the Disciples

"Follow me, and I will make you fishers of men."(Matthew 4:19)

Meditation: Jesus calls ordinary people into extraordinary vocations.

Reflection: Can I trust that what God invites me into will be meaningful and good, even if it's unfamiliar?

Affirmation: "I say yes to divine invitations."

4th Mystery - Mary's Fiat

> "Let it be done to me according to your word." (Luke 1:38)

Meditation: Mary trusted God with her future. Her surrender led to the world's salvation.

Reflection: Where can I say yes to God's plan, even in uncertainty?

Affirmation: "I offer my yes with faith."

5th Mystery - Jesus in the Temple

> "Did you not know I must be in my Father's house?" (Luke 2:49)

Meditation: Even as a youth, Jesus was clear about his purpose. God wants you to know yours too.

Reflection: Where do I feel most alive, called, and gifted to serve?

Affirmation: "I seek to be about God's business."

Closing Prayer

Jesus, just as you called your disciples and guided your earthly parents with clarity and love, lead me in the direction that honors you and fulfills my purpose.

Mary, Seat of Wisdom, be my intercessor and compass.

Help me to discern with peace, courage, and deep trust. May I walk forward with hope, knowing I am never alone.

Amen.

Transitioning to a New Field or Industry

For those in the midst of a career change

Opening Prayer

Our Lady of the Way, so true, guide me in all I seek to do.

This path is new, I'm filled with fear, but with your grace, I'll persevere.

A new dream calls, a fresh begun, lead me as you led your Son.

To what is fruitful, pure, and right, directed always by your light.

With courage strong, I'll take each stride, bless every step, stay by my side.

Amen.

1st Mystery - Abraham's Journey to a New Land

"Go to the land that I will show you."(Genesis 12:1)

Meditation: Sometimes God doesn't reveal the whole map - only the next step.

Reflection: Am I willing to move forward with faith, even without full clarity?

Affirmation: "I trust the journey, even when the road is new."

2nd Mystery - Peter Leaves His Nets

"They left everything and followed Him." (Luke 5:11)

Meditation: Leaving what's familiar can be the start of true transformation.

Reflection: What am I clinging to that is keeping me from growth?

Affirmation: "I release the old to embrace the new."

3rd Mystery - God Does a New Thing

"See, I am doing a new thing! Do you not perceive it?" (Isaiah 43:19)

Meditation: Transitions are invitations to trust that God is making a way.

Reflection: Am I recognizing the new path opening before me, or resisting it?

Affirmation: "I perceive and receive the new thing God is doing."

4th Mystery - Paul's Reinvention

"At once he began to preach... that Jesus is the Son of God."(Acts 9:20)

Meditation: Paul's entire life pivoted toward a new mission. Reinvention is sacred.

Reflection: What part of my past can become fuel for a new calling?

Affirmation: "My past is not wasted - it's being transformed."

5th Mystery - The Wind of the Spirit

"The wind blows wherever it pleases. You hear its sound... but you cannot tell where it comes from or where it is going."(John 3:8)

Meditation: Sometimes God moves like the wind - wild, unseen, yet deeply purposeful.

Reflection: Can I trust what I cannot see

Affirmation: "I go where the Spirit leads me."

Closing Prayer

Holy Spirit, stir within me the faith to step into this new chapter with grace.

Open the doors that are aligned with my purpose, and close the ones that will no longer serve me.

Mary, Mother of Pilgrims, walk beside me as I enter unfamiliar ground. May I move forward not with fear, but with freedom.

Amen.

Job Dissatisfaction

For Those Who Don't Like Their Work

Opening Prayer

Our Lady of Perpetual Help, I come to you feeling drained, frustrated, and unseen.

Work has become heavy - not holy. I ask for your help in finding peace where I am or finding the courage to leave when the time is right.

Give me hope in this season, grace to endure, and clarity to see the blessings hidden in my labor.

Amen.

1st Mystery - The Israelites in Egypt

"They made their lives bitter with hard labor..."(Exodus 1:14)

Meditation: God sees when the work becomes oppressive and He moves to free His people.

Reflection: Am I honest with God about how heavy this job feels?

Affirmation: "God hears my groans and sees my struggle."

2nd Mystery - Jesus Carries the Cross

"They seized Simon...and laid the cross on him to carry."(Luke 23:26)

Meditation: Sometimes we are asked to carry a burden that feels like someone else's. Even then, it has meaning.

Reflection: Where am I carrying more than I was meant to carry?

Affirmation: "My struggle is not invisible to Heaven."

3rd Mystery Joseph in Prison

"But the Lord was with Joseph and showed him steadfast love."(Genesis 39:20-21)

Meditation: Even in unfair circumstances, Joseph prospered through God's presence.

Reflection: How can I invite God into this workplace, even if it feels like a prison?

Affirmation: "God is with me in this place."

4th Mystery - Paul and Silas Sing in Jail

> "About midnight, Paul and Silas were praying and singing hymns..."(Acts 16:25)

Meditation: Praise in dark places breaks chains.

Reflection: How can I shift my focus to gratitude without denying my pain?

Affirmation: "I can choose peace in this season."

5th Mystery - The Beatitudes at Work

> "Blessed are those who are persecuted... for theirs is the kingdom of heaven."(Matthew 5:10)

Meditation: Even difficult jobs can sanctify us.

Reflection: What virtue is this job helping me develop - even through difficulty?

Affirmation: "God is shaping me even here."

Closing Prayer

Jesus, be my co-worker.

Walk with me through the tension and the weariness. Give me wisdom: whether to stay or to go.

And if I stay, give me the grace to bloom even in rocky soil.

Mother Mary, show me how to make this work holy. Hold me close until joy returns.

Amen.

Burnout and Overwhelm

For Those Experiencing Burnout and Overwhelm

Opening Prayer

Mother Mary, hear my plea,

I'm worn, stretched thin, and it's hard to see. you stood by the Cross, so brave, so true, you know the trials I'm walking through.

I bring my burnout to your care, for rest, renewal, a lifted prayer.

Grant me grace in all I do, and strength to see each moment through.

Amen.

1st Mystery - Elijah Under the Broom Tree

> "He lay down and slept under a broom tree... 'It is enough now, O Lord, take away my life.'"(1 Kings 19:4)

Meditation: Even prophets become overwhelmed. Even saints break down. God meets us in the collapse.

Reflection: Have I honored my limits or tried to live without them?

Affirmation: "God meets me in my exhaustion, not just my effort."

2nd Mystery - Jesus Sleeps in the Storm

> "But He was in the stern, asleep on a cushion."(Mark 4:38)

Meditation: Rest is not weakness. Even Jesus paused-in the chaos - to renew.

Reflection: Where do I need permission to rest, even when the world is spinning?

Affirmation: "I can rest, even in the storm."

3rd Mystery - Martha's Worry, Mary's Rest

> "Martha, Martha, you are anxious and troubled... Mary has chosen the better part."(Luke 10:41-42)

Meditation: Productivity is not proof of worth. Presence is the better gift.

Reflection: Am I caught in doing when I am called to be?

Affirmation: "I am valuable even when I'm not producing."

4th Mystery - Come to Me, All Who Are Weary

> "Come to me, all you who labor and are heavy laden, and I will give you rest." (Matthew 11:28)

Meditation: Rest is sacred. Restoration is a promise.

Reflection: Am I allowing Jesus to carry what I was never meant to hold alone?

Affirmation: "I accept divine rest and release the weight."

5th Mystery - Renewal Through the Spirit

> "Those who wait upon the Lord shall renew their strength." (Isaiah 40:31)

Meditation: Renewal is real. The soul can rise again.

Reflection: Am I creating space to be renewed - body, mind, and soul?

Affirmation: "I will rise again, restored by the Spirit."

Closing Prayer

Jesus, I give You my burnout. My fatigue. My pressure. My tears. I am tired of pushing through.

Breathe into me, Spirit of Life. Make space in me for peace. Holy Mary, bearer of sorrows and quiet strength, wrap me in your mantle.

Teach me the rhythm of grace: work that flows from love, not depletion.

Amen.

Financial Provision Through Work

For those desiring more money

Opening Prayer

Mother Mary, Our Lady of Divine Providence, I come with open hands and a weary heart.

I desire to work, to provide, to thrive - not just survive. You who interceded for the wedding feast at Cana, and who carried Jesus through poverty and exile, understand my worry.

Help me to place my finances in God's hands while honoring the dignity of labor.

May I see the fruit of my work and not be left in lack.

Amen.

1st Mystery - The Widow's Jar of Oil

"The oil stopped flowing when there were no more jars." (2 Kings 4:6)

Meditation: Provision flows when we make space for it sometimes miraculously.

Reflection: Am I open to unexpected means of provision and creative income?

Affirmation: "My needs are seen, and my jar will be filled."

2nd Mystery - Jesus Feeds the Five Thousand

> "He gave thanks and distributed... as much as they wanted."(John 6:11)

Meditation: What looks like lack can become abundance in God's hands.

Reflection: Am I withholding my gifts because they seem too small?

Affirmation: "What I have is enough for God to multiply."

3rd Mystery - The Laborers in the Vineyard

> "Am I not allowed to do what I choose with what belongs to me?"(Matthew 20:14-15)

Meditation: God's provision is not always according to our expectations - but it is always just.

Reflection: Am I comparing my provision to others, or trusting my portion?

Affirmation: "God's provision for me is personal and perfect."

4th Mystery - Peter's Coin in the Fish

> "Take the first fish you catch... you will find a coin."(Matthew 17:27)

Meditation: God can bring resources from the most unlikely places.

Reflection: Where might provision be hiding that I've overlooked?

Affirmation: "I am open to provision beyond logic."

5th Mystery - The Daily Bread

> "Give us this day our daily bread."(Matthew 6:11)

Meditation: God does not always give us excess - but He always gives enough.

Reflection: Can I find peace with being sustained one day at a time?

Affirmation: "Today, I will have enough."

Closing Prayer

Lord, You are the giver of all good things.

Provide for me not only financially, but emotionally and spiritually.

Bless the work of my hands. Open the windows of Heaven and pour out what I need. And if the doors seem closed, show me the window. Mary,

Mother of Providence, guide me with your calm faith and unwavering trust. I surrender scarcity for the abundance of grace.

Amen.

Discovering Your Vocation or Purpose

For Those Unsure of Their Calling

Opening Prayer

Mother Mary, you said "yes" with faith before you could see the full path.

I come to you now unsure of what I am called to do, yet longing to live a life that reflects God's dream for me.

Walk with me, Mary, as I search for meaning, for purpose, and for alignment with my soul's true work. Help me hear God's voice and respond with trust.

Amen.

1st Mystery - Jeremiah's Calling

"Before I formed you in the womb I knew you; before you were born I set you apart."(Jeremiah 1:5)

Meditation: Your life has purpose, woven into you from the beginning.

Reflection: What has always been true about me - even as a child?

Affirmation: "I was created with purpose and intention."

2nd Mystery - The Annunciation

"Behold, I am the handmaid of the Lord."(Luke 1:38)

Meditation: Mary's purpose began with surrender. So does ours.

Reflection: Am I open to the purpose God is offering me - even if it's unexpected?

Affirmation: "I say yes to God's calling."

3rd Mystery - Jesus Reads the Scroll

"The Spirit of the Lord is upon me, because he has anointed me to bring good News..." (Luke 4:18)

Meditation: Jesus knew who He was and what He was anointed to do. You can too.

Reflection: Where do I feel called to bring light, healing, or truth?

Affirmation: "I am anointed for something sacred."

4th Mystery - The Body Has Many Parts

"God arranged the members in the body... as he chose." (1 Corinthians 12:18)

Meditation: Your purpose may not look like anyone else's. It doesn't need to.

Reflection: Am I embracing my unique gifts or comparing myself to others?

Affirmation: "I am needed in the Body of Christ."

5th Mystery - Paul Finishes the Race

"I have fought the good fight, I have finished the race, I have kept the faith." (2 Timothy 4:7)

Meditation: Your calling is not just about beginning well - but about finishing faithful.

Reflection: What small step can I take today toward living out my purpose?

Affirmation: "I will walk in purpose, one step at a time."

Closing Prayer

Holy Spirit, I open myself to the purpose You have for my life. Unfold it before me like the dawn.

Help me to listen, to discern, and to walk forward without fear.

Mary, first disciple and mother of vocation, pray for me as I seek to live in alignment with Heaven's design for me.

Amen.

New Job or Opportunity

For those wanting new financial options

Opening Prayer

Mother Mary, Our Lady of Prompt Succor, I come to you with a hopeful and humble heart.

You who hasten to the aid of those in need - intercede for me now. I ask for doors to open, for favor to be shown, and for divine timing to guide every application, interview, and conversation.

Walk beside me as I search, prepare, and wait in trust.

Amen.

1st Mystery - Ruth Finds Favor

"Why have I found such favor in your eyes?" (Ruth 2:10)

Meditation: Ruth's faithfulness led her to a field of unexpected favor. God sees your perseverance.

Reflection: Where have I been faithful, even without recognition?

Affirmation: "I will be guided to where I am seen and valued."

2nd Mystery - Elijah Fed by Ravens

"The ravens brought him bread and meat morning and evening..."(1 Kings 17:6)

Meditation: God provides in miraculous ways when we follow His lead.

Reflection: Am I open to unexpected forms of provision?

Affirmation: "Provision will find me where God sends me."

3rd Mystery The Open Door

"Behold, I have set before you an open door, which no one is able to shut." (Revelation 3:8)

Meditation: Trust that what is meant for you will not pass you by.

Reflection: Am I clinging to closed doors instead of stepping through the one before me?

Affirmation: "I walk through the door God opens for me."

4th Mystery - Joseph is Raised to Leadership

> "Pharaoh said... I hereby put you in charge of the whole land of Egypt." (Genesis 41:41)

Meditation: Joseph's long preparation led to sudden promotion.

Reflection: Can I trust the delays have been forming me for what's next?

Affirmation: "My preparation is not in vain."

5th Mystery - The Good Shepherd Leads

> "He leads me beside still waters... He guides me in paths of righteousness." (Psalm 23:2-3)

Meditation: God's guidance brings peace, not pressure.

Reflection: Am I seeking peace as confirmation of the right path?

Affirmation: "I will be led with peace and purpose."

Closing Prayer

Lord, I lift up my work, my hopes, and my uncertainty to You.

You know where I belong, where my gifts will flourish, and where I will find joy in serving.

Lead me to the place where I am needed and where I can grow.

Mary, swift in compassion and strong in intercession, bring me quickly to the opportunity prepared for me.

Amen.

Entrepreneurial Courage and Wisdom

For those wanting to work for themselves

Opening Prayer

O Lord, our guide, so strong and true, we humbly lift our hearts to You.

Grant us wisdom, courage, and peace, that in this venture, joy may increase.

For dreams we chase and risks we take, bless every step that we do make.

Through trials and triumphs, light our way, and help us trust You every day.

With grace from You, we seek to grow, to build and serve where seeds we sow.

Protect our cause, O Lord above, and fill our work with boundless love.

Amen.

1st Mystery - Noah Builds the Ark

"So Noah did everything just as God commanded him." (Genesis 6:14-22)

Meditation: Noah trusted in God's vision, even when it didn't make sense to others. Building the ark required faith, patience, and obedience. Consider the areas in your life where God may be calling you to step out in faith, even if it feels uncertain. Trust that His blueprint is perfect.

Reflection: Am I willing to build what no one else sees yet?

Affirmation: "I build with heaven's blueprint."

2nd Mystery - Proverbs on Diligence

"Do you see a man skillful in his work? He will stand before kings." (Proverbs 22:29)

Meditation: Excellence attracts opportunity. When we commit to growing our skills and working with diligence, we reflect God's creativity and purpose. Take a moment to reflect on how you can refine your craft and offer your work as an act of worship.

Reflection: "Am I cultivating skill and excellence?"

Affirmation: "My diligence opens doors."

3rd Mystery - The Woman with the Oil Business

"She perceives her merchandise is profitable."(Proverbs 31:18)

Meditation: Believing in the value of what we create is vital to blessing others. This woman's confidence in her God-given abilities allowed her to thrive. Reflect on how you see the work of your hands- do you trust that what you're offering can serve and bless others?

Reflection: Do I believe in the value of what I offer?

Affirmation: "My work blesses others."

4th Mystery - Jesus the Carpenter

"Is this not the carpenter...?" (Mark 6:3)

Meditation: Jesus honored His craft, using His hands to build with care and purpose. All work, no matter how small, can be sacred when done with love and devotion. Consider how you can invite God into your daily tasks and honor Him through your work.

Reflection: Am I honoring the sacred in my craft?

Affirmation: "My hands do holy work."

5th Mystery - The Builders of the Temple

"The temple was built with stone finished at the quarry..."(1 Kings 6:7)

Meditation: Building something meaningful requires preparation and dedication. The temple was built with precision and care, reflecting eternal purpose. Reflect on what you are building in your life-are you laying down a lasting foundation for the future??

Reflection: Am I building something that will last?

Affirmation: "I create with eternal vision."

Closing Prayer

Our Lady of Good Counsel,

Guide us with Your wisdom and intercede for us as we navigate the challenges ahead.

Grant us courage, humility, and perseverance to follow God's will in all we do. May our work honor Him, serve others faithfully, and be a true blessing to those we encounter.

Pray for us, that we may always seek His guidance, trust in His timing, and strive to bring joy and hope through our efforts.

Amen.

Balancing Work and Family

For those wanting a healthy balance of work and family life

Opening Prayer

Loving Mother Mary, we come before you seeking your guidance and intercession as we strive to balance the demands of work and family life.

Teach us to embrace simplicity, to prioritize what truly matters, and to love with the same tenderness and devotion you showed to Jesus.

Be our model of patience, strength, and grace as we reflect on these mysteries of faith.

Amen.

1st Mystery - Martha and Mary

"You are worried and upset about many things..." (Luke 10:41-42)

Meditation: Reflect on the importance of slowing down and being present with God. Consider how often busyness distracts from what truly matters.

Reflection: Am I placing presence above productivity?

Affirmation: "I choose what matters most."

2nd Mystery - The Holy Family's Simplicity

"His mother treasured all these things in her heart." (Luke 2:51)

Meditation: Reflect on the simplicity and humility of the Holy Family. Consider how they found holiness in their everyday lives, embracing love, trust, and faith in even the most ordinary moments.

Reflection: Do I honor the sacred in my daily life?

Affirmation: "My home is my holy ground."

3rd Mystery - Jesus Blesses the Children

"Let the little children come to me..." (Mark 10:14)

Meditation: Reflect on the purity, trust, and simplicity of a child's heart, and consider how you can embrace these qualities in your own relationships and daily life.

Reflection: "How can I make space for joy and tenderness?"

Affirmation: I give my loved ones my best.

4th Mystery - Proverbs on Rest

"When you lie down, your sleep will be sweet." (Proverbs 3:24)

Meditation: Consider the gift of rest as a way to renew your mind, body, and spirit. Reflect on how rest allows you to trust in God's care and provision, letting go of worries and embracing peace.

Reflection: Am I honoring my need for rest?

Affirmation: "Rest is holy."

5th Mystery - Jesus Heals Peter's Mother-in-Law

"She got up and began to serve Him." (Matthew 8:15)

Meditation: Reflect on how Jesus's healing empowers us to rise and serve others with love. Consider the ways He restores you, inviting you to serve not out of obligation but out of gratitude and joy.

Reflection: Am I serving from love, not pressure?

Affirmation: "I serve with joy, not depletion."

Closing Prayer

Loving God, we come to you seeking your wisdom and strength as we navigate the balance between our work and our family.

Help us to remain rooted in love, guided by your example of care and compassion.

Teach us to prioritize what is sacred-time spent with loved ones, moments of rest, and the joy of simple, meaningful connections.

Grant us patience in challenges, clarity in decisions, and the grace to serve from a place of love, not exhaustion.

May our homes be filled with peace, our work with purpose, and our hearts with gratitude for the blessings you have entrusted to us.

Amen.

Students and Vocational Training

For those preparing themselves for work

Opening Prayer

Heavenly Father,

We come before You with grateful hearts, seeking Your guidance and wisdom as we journey through our studies, training, and work.

Bless us with mental clarity to grasp the knowledge we need and the strength to persevere in every challenge.

May Your Spirit guide our learning, helping us grow in understanding, humility, and purpose.

Inspire us to use our gifts for the good of others and to glorify You in all that we do. We entrust our efforts and ambitions to Your care, trusting in Your divine plan for our lives.

Amen.

1st Mystery - The Boy Jesus in the Temple

"They found Him sitting among the teachers..." (Luke 2:46-47)

Meditation: Picture the young Jesus, eager to learn, asking questions, and engaging with the teachers. His hunger for wisdom reminds us of the importance of seeking knowledge with both curiosity and humility.

Reflection: Do I seek wisdom eagerly and humbly?

Affirmation: I am teachable and growing.

2nd Mystery - Proverbs on Knowledge

"Let the wise listen and add to their learning."(Proverbs 1:5)

Meditation: Reflect on the invitation to listen and grow. Wisdom is not static; it's a journey of continued learning and openness to understanding more each day.

Reflection: How can I commit to deep learning today?

Affirmation: I grow in knowledge and favor.

3rd Mystery - Solomon's Prayer for Wisdom

"Give your servant a discerning heart..."(1 Kings 3:9)

Meditation: Imagine Solomon humbly asking God for wisdom, not for his own gain, but to serve others better. His example challenges us to seek wisdom with pure intentions.

Reflection: What kind of wisdom do I truly need?

Affirmation: "I ask for divine understanding."

4th Mystery Paul's Studies Under Gamaliel

"I was thoroughly trained in the law..."(Acts 22:3)

Meditation: Consider Paul's dedication to his studies and how his preparation later helped him fulfill his mission. Excellence in learning can equip us to make a greater impact.

Reflection: Am I committed to excellence in my field?

Affirmation: "I honor my training as preparation."

5th Mystery - The Spirit Teaches All Things

"The Holy Spirit will teach you all things..."(John 14:26)

Meditation: Envision the Holy Spirit guiding you, illuminating truths, and shaping your understanding. Trust that divine teaching is always available to you.

Reflection: Am I allowing God to shape my learning journey?

Affirmation: "The Spirit helps me learn."

Closing Prayer

As we continue our journey through studies, training, and work, may the seeds of wisdom You have planted in our hearts grow and bear fruit in our lives.

Grant us the courage to face challenges with faith, the perseverance to pursue excellence, and the humility to always seek Your guidance.

Help us use the knowledge and skills we gain to serve others and glorify You in all we do. We entrust our future to Your loving care, confident in Your plans for us.

Amen.

Workplace Justice and Ethical Leadership

For those wanting to improve the culture of their workplace or work

Opening Prayer

Heavenly Father, hear our plea, for justice, peace, and equity.

In work and labor, may we find, your guiding hand, both just and kind.

Bless those who strive with heart and grace, to build a fair and holy place.

For equal pay and rightful care, may we reflect Your love and share.

Grant us courage, bold and true, to seek what's right in all we do.

In every task, both great and small, may we honor You, who leads us all.

Amen.

1st Mystery - Moses Confronts Pharaoh

"Let my people go." (Exodus 5:1)

Meditation: Picture Moses standing before Pharaoh, filled with courage and conviction. Imagine the strength it took to demand freedom for his people. Visualize the power of speaking truth to authority and the ripple effect it can create.

Reflection: Where am I called to speak up for others?

Affirmation: "I use my voice for justice."

2nd Mystery - Jesus Clears the Temple

"My Father's house... a house of prayer!" (John 2:15-16)

Meditation: Envision the moment Jesus walks into the temple, filled with righteous anger for what it had become. Reflect on His unwavering commitment to preserve what is sacred. Consider how you can bring that same clarity and conviction into your own spaces.

Reflection: How can I keep my workplace sacred?

Affirmation: "I protect what is holy."

3rd Mystery The Beatitudes

"Blessed are those who hunger for righteousness..." (Matthew 5:6)

Meditation: Imagine standing on the hill, hearing Jesus proclaim the Beatitudes. Feel the call to live a life of integrity, justice, and compassion. Reflect on the deep hunger for righteousness that can guide your actions and decisions.

Reflection: Am I living out kingdom values at work?

Affirmation: "I hunger for what is right."

4th Mystery - Nehemiah Rebuilds with Integrity

"I am doing a great work and I cannot come down." (Nehemiah 6:3)

Meditation: Picture Nehemiah standing firm in the face of distraction and opposition. Reflect on the importance of staying committed to your mission, even when challenges arise. Imagine the strength and focus it takes to lead with integrity.

Reflection: Am I staying focused despite resistance?

Affirmation: "I lead with focus and courage."

5th Mystery - The Good Samaritan

"He took pity on him.."(Luke 10:33)

Meditation: Visualize the Samaritan stopping to care for the injured man, setting aside his plans to show mercy and compassion. Reflect on the power of small acts of kindness and how they can transform someone's life. Consider how you can bring this compassion into your leadership or work.

Reflection: How can I bring compassion into my leadership or work?

Affirmation: "I lead with mercy."

Closing Prayer

O Lord, we thank You, hear our call, for justice, fairness and love for all.

In every workplace, great or small, may kindness reign and hatred fall.

We trust in You, Your guiding light, to lead us through the darkest night.

Where equity and peace seem rare, remind us, Lord, that You are there.

With hearts united, strong and true, we strive for what is right and new.

A world where all can safely stand, together built by Your own hand.

Let mercy, fairness, shape our way, and goodness triumph every day.

For in Your love, all hope remains, till justice flows like endless rains.

Amen.

12

Rosaries for Parents

"All your children will be taught by the Lord, and great will be their peace." - Isaiah 54:13

Parenthood is a beautiful and profound experience, but it is also filled with countless mysteries. From the moment a child is born, parents find themselves navigating a world of questions, uncertainties, and wonders that often have no clear answers. These mysteries span the emotional, physical, and mental aspects of parenting, making the journey both challenging and rewarding. These mysteries are intricately woven into the fabric of parenthood, guiding parents through the challenging and joyous moments from pregnancy to postpartum and beyond.

During pregnancy, the physical changes and emotional shifts prepare parents to nurture a new life, even if the path feels uncertain. The postpartum phase, filled with sleepless nights and new routines, challenges parents to adapt, trust their instincts, and seek support when needed. As children grow, the questions and milestones evolve, but so do the opportunities for connection, learning, and growth.

Though challenging, these mysteries are designed to foster resilience, patience, and an unyielding bond between parent and child, shaping the parenting experience into one of profound discovery and love. Through these mysteries, parents can journey deeper into the graces of care, compassion, and strength, drawing inspiration from the example of Mother Mary and her unwavering love for Jesus.

Devotion to Our Lady of La Leche

For mothers seeking grace, strength, and divine guidance in their sacred role

Opening Prayer

To You, lovely Lady of La Leche, and to your Divine Son, do I now dedicate this little baby whom our Father in heaven has given me.

Grateful for the trust He has placed in me, I beg you to obtain for me the physical and spiritual graces I need to fulfill my duties at every moment.

Amen.

1st Mystery: The Nativity of Jesus (The Gift of Life)

"And she gave birth to her firstborn son and wrapped him in swaddling cloths and laid him in a manger, because there was no place for them in the inn."(Luke 2:7)

Meditation: Reflect on the miracle of life and the sacred trust of motherhood. Pray for the grace to nurture and protect the life entrusted to you, just as Mary cared for the infant Jesus.

Reflection: In the humblest of settings, God chose to enter the world, reminding us that even in our simplest moments, we can experience profound joy and purpose. The Nativity teaches us that love and care, no matter the circumstances, can make any place holy.

Affirmation: "I will honor the gift of life, cherishing each moment as a blessing. I am committed to nurturing others with love, patience, and compassion, just as Mary nurtured Jesus."

2nd Mystery: The Presentation in the Temple (Offering Your Child to God)

> "When the time came for their purification according to the Law of Moses, they brought him up to Jerusalem to present him to the Lord." (Luke 2:22)

Meditation: Like Mary and Joseph presenting Jesus in the temple, offer your child to God's loving care. Pray for the wisdom to guide your child in faith and love, trusting in God's plan for their life.

Reflection: As parents, we are stewards of the precious lives God has entrusted to us. The act of presenting our children to the Lord is a reminder that they ultimately belong to Him. Reflect on how you can nurture their gifts and guide them to fulfill the purpose God has set for them.

Affirmation: "Lord, I trust in Your divine plan for my child. I surrender my fears and anxieties, knowing that You will guide their steps and surround them with Your love and protection."

3rd Mystery: The Flight into Egypt (Protection in Times of Trial)

"And he rose and took the child and his mother by night and departed to Egypt."(Matthew 2:14)

Meditation: Reflect on Mary's courage and trust as she fled to protect her child. Pray for strength and guidance in times of uncertainty, and for the protection of your family from harm.

Reflection: In times of trial, we are reminded of the power of trust and faith. Just as Mary and Joseph relied on God's guidance to navigate their journey, we too can find strength in surrendering our fears to a higher purpose. Challenges can become opportunities for growth and deeper faith when we trust in God's plan.

Affirmation: "I trust in God's protection and guidance, even in uncertain times. My family and I are surrounded by divine care and love, and we will find strength and peace in every trial we face."

4th Mystery: The Wedding at Cana (Trusting in Mary's Intercession)

"When the wine ran out, the mother of Jesus said to him, 'They have no wine.' And Jesus said to her, 'Woman, what does this have to do with me? My hour has not yet come.' His mother said to the servants, 'Do whatever he tells you.'" (John 2:3-5)

Meditation: Trust in Mary's intercession, just as she interceded at Cana. Pray for her to obtain the graces you need as a mother, and for her guidance in moments of doubt or difficulty.

Reflection: Just as Mary noticed the need at the wedding feast and brought it to Jesus, she notices our needs and brings them to Him with love and care. Her confidence in Jesus' power reminds us to trust fully in God's timing, even when we do not understand His plans.

Affirmation: "I trust in Mary's intercession and place my faith in Jesus' ability to work all things for good. I will look to Mary's example of trust and confidently surrender my needs to God."

5th Mystery: The Crucifixion and Mary at the Foot of the Cross (Strength in Suffering)

"Standing by the cross of Jesus were his mother and his mother's sister, Mary the wife of Clopas, and Mary Magdalene. When Jesus saw his mother and the disciple whom he loved standing nearby, he said to his mother, 'Woman, behold, your son!' Then he said to the disciple, 'Behold, your mother!'" (John 19:25-27)

Meditation: Reflect on Mary's strength and faith as she stood by the cross. Pray for the grace to endure the challenges of motherhood with courage and trust, knowing that Mary walks with you in your trials.

Reflection: In the face of unimaginable suffering, Mary remained steadfast in her faith and trust in God's plan. Her silent strength is a reminder that even in our darkest moments, God's love surrounds us. By offering her Son to the world, Mary teaches us the true meaning of surrender and love.

Affirmation: I will face my struggles with courage and faith, trusting that God's love will guide me. Like Mary, I will remain steadfast, knowing I am never alone in my suffering.

Closing Prayer

"To You, lovely Lady of La Leche, and to your Divine Son, do I now dedicate this little baby whom our Father in heaven has given me.

Grateful for the trust He has placed in me, I beg you to obtain for me the physical and spiritual graces I need to fulfill my duties at every moment."

Amen.

Breastfeeding

For those who are grieving, struggling with, or seeking healing around the experience of not being able to breastfeed

Opening Prayer

O Sorrowful and Immaculate Heart of Mary,

Mother of all who suffer in silence, draw near to me in my longing and tears.

You held the lifeless body of your Son in your arms —you understand a mother's pain.

Hold my heart and transform it with your tenderness.

Help me unite my loss with yours, that I may be filled with divine comfort and peace.

Amen.

1st Sorrow: The Prophecy of Simeon

"A sword will pierce your own soul too." Luke 2:35

Meditation: Sometimes we feel the sting of a hidden sword — invisible to others, yet sharp. The loss of breastfeeding is not just physical — it is emotional, spiritual, ancestral.

Reflection: This is not your fault. Your body is sacred, not broken. Your motherhood is not diminished.

Affirmation: "I honor my body and trust that love is enough. I am still whole."

2nd Sorrow: The Flight into Egypt

"Take the child and his mother and flee..." Matthew 2:13–14

Meditation: Running from danger with a newborn is a deep fear. When feeding doesn't work, it can feel like you're constantly escaping judgment, shame, or failure.

Reflection: Even in the wilderness, God provided. This journey will bring hidden blessings.

Affirmation: "I am protected. I am being guided to nourishment in new ways."

3rd Sorrow: The Loss of the Child Jesus in the Temple

"Child, why have you treated us like this?" Luke 2:48

Meditation: Losing what you hoped for in early motherhood — like the bond through breastfeeding — feels like losing part of yourself.

Reflection: Mary, too, searched for what was lost. God restores in mysterious ways.

Affirmation: "I will find new ways to connect, nourish, and thrive as a mother."

4th Sorrow: Mary Meets Jesus on the Way to Calvary

"Daughters of Jerusalem, do not weep for me…" Luke 23:27–28

Meditation: Seeing your child suffer — even with minor discomforts — is agony. Breastfeeding struggles can feel like failing to soothe.

Reflection: Mary saw suffering and could not stop it, but she walked with Him. So do you.

Affirmation: "I accompany my child with love. That is enough."

5th Sorrow: The Crucifixion and Death of Jesus

"Woman, behold your son." John 19:26–27

Meditation: Death of expectations. Death of dreams. This sorrow is sacred. A kind of crucifixion.

Reflection: Mary didn't leave the cross. She stayed and bore witness. Your grief is not too much.

Affirmation: "I make room for grief and resurrection. I am loved in the depths of my sorrow."

Closing Prayer

Mother of Sorrows, you who bore the weight of divine mystery and the ache of maternal loss, carry me now.

Help me see that I am not alone. That my pain is held in your mantle.

May I mother from a place of presence, not pressure.

From the heart, not performance.

Amen.

Post Partum

For mothers navigating postpartum changes and learning to trust the process

Opening Prayer

Mother Mary, full of grace, guide us in this tender space.

Through sleepless nights and days unknown, help us see how love has grown.

Give us strength when we feel weak, your gentle wisdom we now seek.

In this season, help us find, peace and trust in heart and mind.

Amen.

1st Mystery: The Annunciation (Accepting the Call)

"Behold, I am the handmaid of the Lord; let it be to me according to your word." (Luke 1:38)

Meditation: Like Mary, you are called into a new season-uncertain but holy. Reflect on the "yes" you're giving now, even without full clarity. Trust that your surrender is sacred and will lead to transformation.

Reflection: Embracing uncertainty can feel daunting, but like Mary, we are reminded that trust in divine guidance opens the door to profound growth and purpose. Your willingness to say "yes" is an act of faith that plants the seeds for transformation, even if the path ahead is unclear.

Affirmation: "I trust in the divine plan for my life. My surrender is sacred, and I am open to the blessings and growth that come with this new season."

2nd Mystery: The Finding of Jesus in the Temple (Seeking Purpose in Transition)

> "Did you not know I must be about my Father's business?" (Luke 2:49)

Meditation: Like Mary searching for Jesus, you too are discerning your path. This mystery honors the tension between holding on and letting go as a mother. Pray for wisdom and peace as you navigate the unknown.

Reflection: Trust that even in times of uncertainty, God is guiding both your steps and the steps of those you love. Just as Mary found Jesus fulfilling His purpose, you will find clarity and purpose as you seek Him in your own journey.

Affirmation: "I release my fears to God and embrace the wisdom and peace He provides. I trust that His plan will unfold in perfect timing."

3rd Mystery: Jesus Takes Up His Cross (Embracing the Weight of Change)

"If anyone would come after me, let him deny himself, take up his cross, and follow me." (Matthew 16:24)

Meditation: Your transition may feel heavy-like Jesus walking to Calvary. Offer your fatigue, fear, or doubt as part of your sacred journey. Trust that every step, no matter how difficult, is leading you closer to transformation.

Reflection: Consider the times in your life when change felt like a burden too heavy to carry. Just as Jesus embraced His cross, you are invited to embrace the challenges of your journey with faith and courage. Each struggle is an opportunity to grow stronger, deepen your trust, and align more closely with your purpose. Remember, transformation often begins with the willingness to carry the weight of change.

Affirmation: "I embrace life's challenges as steps toward my growth and transformation. With every burden I carry, I trust that I am being guided toward greater strength, purpose, and peace."

4th Mystery: The Assumption of Mary (Being Lifted Up)

"Arise, my love, my beautiful one, and come away." (Song of Solomon 2:10)

Meditation: Like Mary, your labor-whether physical, emotional, or spiritual-will not end in decay but ascension. Trust that God is lifting you even now, carrying you toward renewal and peace.

Reflection: Consider the ways God has carried you through challenges and lifted you toward moments of growth and grace. Just as Mary was assumed into heaven, reflect on how your faith invites you to rise above struggles and embrace God's promise of renewal.

Affirmation: "I trust in God's plan to lift me toward peace, renewal, and fulfillment. In His hands, I rise above all challenges."

5th Mystery: The Coronation of Mary (Your Glory to Come)

> "You are clothed with strength and dignity; you can laugh at the days to come." (Proverbs 31:25)

Meditation: Imagine your future self-crowned, radiant, and at peace. This is your promise: What feels like an ending is a birthing. Trust that your journey will lead to glory, and you will emerge stronger and more whole.

Reflection: Life's challenges often feel like endings, but they are pathways to transformation. Trusting in the journey allows us to embrace the promise of strength and dignity that lies ahead. Each step, no matter how difficult, leads us closer to the radiant glory we are destined for.

Affirmation: "I am clothed with strength and dignity. I trust the process of my journey and know that every challenge shapes me into the person I am meant to become. My future is filled with peace, purpose, and glory."

Closing Prayer

Heavenly Mother, guide us with your gentle hands as we walk through life's trials and triumphs.

Teach us to trust in God's divine plan and to carry ourselves with the same strength and grace that you have shown us.

Wrap us in your mantle of love, and help us to always find peace in the promises of Christ.

May our hearts remain steadfast in faith, and may we continue to grow in dignity and love as we follow your perfect example.

Amen.

The Loss of a Child

For those who have lost a child in utero or after birth

Opening Prayer

Heavenly Father, we bring before you the deep grief and pain of losing a beloved child.

We ask for your boundless mercy to comfort our aching hearts. Transform our sorrow into hope through the promise of eternal life in your Son, Jesus Christ.

Strengthen us to trust in your divine purpose, even amid our suffering. Grant us peace and fill us with the assurance that our precious child rests in your loving care, surrounded by eternal joy and light.

Amen.

1st Mystery: The Agony in the Garden

"He withdrew about a stone's throw beyond them, knelt down and prayed, "Father, if you are willing, take this cup from me; yet not my will, but yours be done." An angel from heaven appeared to him and strengthened him.

> And being in anguish, he prayed more earnestly, and his sweat was like drops of blood falling to the ground.." (Luke 22:41-44)

Meditation: Reflect on Christ's acceptance of His suffering and unite your pain with His, trusting that He walks alongside you in your grief.

Reflection: Jesus experienced profound sorrow and anguish in the Garden of Gethsemane, knowing the suffering that lay ahead. Just as He prayed, "Father, if you are willing, take this cup from me; yet not my will, but yours be done" (Luke 22:42), we too turn to God in our darkest hours, submitting to His divine will even when the burden feels unbearable.

Affirmation: "Lord, help us to surrender our sorrow to Your will. Through Your grace, may we find strength to endure and hope in Your eternal plan."

2nd Mystery: The Scourging at the Pillar

> "Then Pilate took Jesus and had him flogged."(John 19:1)

Meditation: Contemplate how Christ bore the weight of every sorrow, including our grief, and allow His love to soothe your broken heart.

Reflection: Every lash Jesus endured was an embodiment of His love for humanity. His suffering reminds us of His deep empathy for every human pain, including the grief of losing a loved one.

Affirmation: "Lord, in the midst of our suffering, may we find consolation in the knowledge that You have shared in our pain and are close to the brokenhearted."

3rd Mystery: The Crowning with Thorns

> "The soldiers twisted together a crown of thorns and put it on his head. They clothed him in a purple robe and went up to him again and again, saying, 'Hail, king of the Jews!' And they slapped him in the face." (John 19:2-3)

Meditation: Ponder Jesus' silent strength and allow His example to inspire a sense of peace in the midst of your sorrow.

Reflection: The crown of thorns placed on Jesus' head mocked His kingship, yet He bore it with dignity and unwavering love. Similarly, while our loss may feel unjust, we are called to trust God's greater purpose.

Affirmation: "Lord, though our hearts are pierced with thorns of grief, we trust in Your promise to redeem and restore. May we wear the crown of faith in Your eternal kingdom."

4th Mystery: The Carrying of the Cross

"As they led him away, they seized Simon of Cyrene, who was on his way in from the country, and put the cross on him and made him carry it behind Jesus."(Luke 23:26)

Meditation: Call to mind Christ's unwavering determination and find comfort in knowing He will give you the strength to bear the weight of loss.

Reflection: Jesus carried the heavy cross to Golgotha, bearing the weight of the world's sin on His shoulders. His perseverance encourages us to carry our own crosses, even in the depths of pain.

Affirmation: "Lord, as we carry the cross of grief, may we feel Your presence lightening our burden and leading us toward Your eternal love."

5th Mystery: The Crucifixion and Death of Jesus

"From noon until three in the afternoon darkness came over all the land. About three in the afternoon Jesus cried out in a loud voice, "Eli, Eli, lema sabachthani?" (which means "My God, my God, why have you forsaken me?"). When some of those standing there heard this, they said, "He's calling Elijah."

> Immediately one of them ran and got a sponge. He filled it with wine vinegar, put it on a staff, and offered it to Jesus to drink. The rest said, "Now leave him alone. Let's see if Elijah comes to save him." And when Jesus had cried out again in a loud voice, he gave up his spirit." (Matthew 27:45-50)

Meditation: Reflect on the hope of resurrection and place your beloved child into God's hands, trusting in the promise of eternal reunion.

Reflection: On the cross, Jesus surrendered His life out of love for us. His death reminds us that God's plan extends beyond the pain of this world to the promise of new life in eternity.

Affirmation: "Lord, as we gaze upon the cross, may we be filled with hope in the glory of the resurrection and the knowledge that death has been defeated by Your love."

Closing Prayer

Loving Father, as we entrust our dearly loved child to Your divine mercy, help us to find peace in Your promise that those who mourn will be comforted.

Strengthen us to carry our grief with faith, and keep our hearts fixed on the hope of eternal life.

May we rest in the assurance that You hold our precious child in Your everlasting arms, safe and surrounded by Your love.

Thank you for walking this difficult path with us and for giving us the gift of Your Son, Jesus Christ, who triumphs over all pain and sorrow. Amen.

Fertility and Family Planning

For those longing to grow their family and are navigating uncertainty, discerning timing, or carrying silent grief

Opening Prayer

Heavenly Father, we come before You with hearts longing for hope and guidance as we navigate the journey of building our families. We entrust our prayers to the intercession of Our Lady seeking comfort, strength, and clarity in times of uncertainty.

For those discerning Your timing, enduring silent grief, or longing to grow their families, we ask for your grace and peace.

As Psalm 113:9 reminds us, "He gives the childless woman a family, making her a happy mother. Praise the Lord!" May this rosary bring us closer to your will and fill our lives with the joy of Your promises.

Amen.

1st Mystery: Hannah's Prayer for a Child

"In her deep anguish Hannah prayed to the Lord, weeping bitterly." (1 Samuel 1:10-11)

Meditation: Hannah's longing was holy. She poured out her soul-not with shame, but faith. God heard. The womb is not forgotten.

Reflection: Have I shared my deepest longings with God - uncensored?

Affirmation: "My longing is sacred. God receives it with compassion."

2nd Mystery: The Annunciation

"'You will conceive and give birth to a son...' Mary said, 'Let it be done to me according to your word.'"(Luke 1:31-38)

Meditation: Mary's yes to life came in mystery. She didn't fully understand - but she trusted. In planning and preparing for family, we also say yes in mystery.

Reflection: Can I surrender control and trust divine timing?

Affirmation: "I welcome life on sacred terms, not fear's timeline."

3rd Mystery: Sarah Bears a Son in Old Age

"The Lord was gracious to Sarah... and she became pregnant."(Genesis 21:1-2)

Meditation: Even laughter of disbelief can turn into laughter of joy. God's timing surpasses biology. Nothing is too hard for Him.

Reflection: Am I willing to believe, even now?

Affirmation: "God can do what I cannot imagine."

4th Mystery: Rachel Cries Out for Children

> "Rachel said, 'Give me children, or I'll die!... Then God remembered Rachel."(Genesis 30:1, 22)

Meditation: Grief and longing can overwhelm- but they are not the end. God remembers. And your tears are prayers.

Reflection: How can I hold space for grief and hope together?

Affirmation: "My sorrow is seen. My story is still unfolding."

5th Mystery: The Holy Family and the Presentation at the Temple

> "They brought Him to Jerusalem to present Him to the Lord..." (Luke 2:22-24)

Meditation: A child is not just a gift - but a calling. Whether by birth, adoption, or spiritual motherhood/fatherhood, we are invited to steward new life with love.

Reflection: Am I open to how God might build family beyond my expectations?

Affirmation: "I am already being made into a vessel of life."

Closing Prayer

Mother of God, you bore divine life in uncertainty and poverty - yet trusted that your yes would change the world.

Bless my longings, my waiting, my choices.

Bless my womb - or the wombs I hold in prayer.

Bless every parent, child, and dream still becoming.

Wrap us in hope.

Amen.

Protecting a Child from Danger

Offering hope and spiritual covering for any caregiver praying for the safety of a beloved child

Opening Prayer

Mary, Queen of Angels, whose mantle covers us in grace, and Guardian Angel, entrusted by God to watch over this child - we come to you with humble hearts, entrusting this little one to your care.

Dearest Guardian Angel, protect them always, shielding them from harm, both seen and unseen.

Go before them with light, defend them in darkness, and guide their every step toward peace and goodness.

Mary, wrap them in your loving embrace, and Guardian Angel, stand ever by their side, that they may grow in faith, love, and the joy of God's presence.

Amen.

1st Mystery - The Escape to Egypt

"An angel of the Lord appeared to Joseph in a dream and said, 'Get up, take the child and his mother, and flee to Egypt... for Herod is about to search for the child, to destroy him."(Matthew 2:13)

Meditation: Close your eyes and imagine Joseph waking in the stillness of the night, the weight of the angel's words heavy on his heart. Picture him quietly gathering Mary and Jesus, trusting in God's guidance despite the unknown. Reflect on how God provides protection and guidance in moments of fear and uncertainty.

Reflection: Even Jesus needed protection. God sent warning through a dream and provided safety through prompt action. When danger looms, Mary and the angels still move in quiet power to guard the innocent.

Affirmation: "No harm shall befall the child under heaven's watch."

2nd Mystery - Daniel in the Lion's Den

"My God sent his angel and shut the lions' mouths so that they would not hurt Me." (Daniel 6:22)

Meditation: Picture Daniel sitting calmly in the lion's den, the creatures resting peacefully around him. Feel the presence of God's angel, a divine shield of protection, surrounding him. Reflect on God's ability to silence the forces of harm in your life and the lives of your loved ones.

Reflection: When a child is in what feels like a lion's den-dangerous environments, bullying, unseen threats-remember: God's angels are near. Their presence shuts the mouths of harm.

Affirmation: "God's angel stands between my child and all harm."

3rd Mystery - Jesus Blesses the Children

> "'Let the little children come to me... for the kingdom of God belongs to such as these.' And He took them in His arms, laid His hands on them, and blessed them." (Mark 10:14,16)

Meditation: Visualize Jesus sitting among children, His arms wide open as they run to Him with joy. Imagine Him gently placing His hands on each child, offering comfort, love, and blessings. Reflect on how Jesus continues to hold and bless your child, even when you cannot.

Reflection: Jesus not only welcomes children, He holds them, blesses them, and covers them. When you cannot be near your child, remember: He still is.

Affirmation: "Jesus embraces and blesses my child always."

4th Mystery - Psalm of Angelic Protection

"For He will command His angels concerning you to guard you in all your ways. They will lift you up in their hands so that you will not strike your foot against a Stone." (Psalm 91:11-12)

Meditation: Envision angels walking beside you and your loved ones, their presence strong and gentle as they guide and protect every step. Reflect on how God's promises of protection bring peace and strength in times of uncertainty.

Reflection: This ancient promise still stands. When we fear, heaven sends guardians. Their hands are under every stumble and every unknown.

Affirmation: "God's angels walk beside my child at every step."

5th Mystery - Peter Rescued by an Angel

"Suddenly an angel of the Lord appeared... and the chains fell off Peter's wrists." (Acts 12:7)

Meditation: Picture Peter in the dark prison, bound in chains, when suddenly a radiant angel appears. Imagine the chains falling away effortlessly and the gates opening. Reflect on how God sends deliverance right when it's needed, breaking through the impossible.

Reflection: When your child feels trapped-by fear, by harm, by confusion—know that angels still enter locked places. Prayer unlocks even what human hands cannot.

Affirmation: "God sends deliverance where I cannot reach."

Closing Prayer

> Mary, Queen of Angels, so pure, wrap this child in a veil secure.
>
> Guardian Angel, gentle and wise, guide their steps, where peace lies.
>
> Go before them, lighting the way, walk beside them every day.
>
> Through your prayers and God's embrace, may they be safe in love and grace
>
> Amen.

13

Rosaries for Family Issues

"Honor your father and your mother, so that you may live long in the land the Lord your God is giving you." — Exodus 20:12

Family is one of the most profound gifts we have, but it is also one of the most complex aspects of our lives. The relationships within a family can bring both extraordinary joy and deep challenges, requiring patience, love, and understanding. Family issues often comprise a range of emotions and experiences that shape who we are, from sibling rivalries and toxic dynamics to feelings of rejection and exclusion as the family outcast.

These dynamics can be difficult to confront, often testing our ability to forgive, reconcile, and remain steadfast in love even when faced with pain or misunderstanding. Forgiveness, in particular, is a central theme in family struggles, as the wounds caused by those closest to us can often cut the deepest. Yet, it is through these challenges that we are called to grow and develop resilience, allowing God's grace to work within us and bring healing to strained relationships.

The following rosaries will help guide you through these family issues, offering a source of strength and reflection during times of conflict, forgiveness, or isolation. By meditating on these mysteries, you can seek peace, unity, and the courage to build or rebuild the bonds that connect you with your loved ones, no matter how strained they may feel.

Patience and Understanding

For those navigating relationship strain or misunderstanding

Opening Prayer

Our Lady of Compassion,

Hold my heart when I want to give up.

Teach me the patience of the Father, the slowness of Christ, and the understanding of those who listen with love.

Make me gentle with others and myself.

Let me grow in empathy and trust.

Amen.

1st Mystery: Sarah Laughs at the Promise

"Sarah laughed to herself... Then the Lord said, 'Is anything too wonderful for the Lord?'"(Genesis 18:12-14)

Meditation: Sarah waited so long, she stopped believing. Impatience can mask despair, but God's timing is deeper and wiser.

Reflection: Where in my life or relationship am I tempted to give up?

Affirmation: "I wait in faith, not fear."

2nd Mystery: The Israelites Grumble in the Desert

> "The whole congregation... grumbled against Moses and Aaron." (Exodus 16:2-3)

Meditation: Patience erodes when we don't trust the journey. The Israelites were freed but still wanted Egypt. Change is hard, but patience trusts God's path.

Reflection: Am I clinging to old comforts instead of trusting God's transformation?

Affirmation: "I trust this journey, even when it feels slow."

3rd Mystery: The Prodigal Son's Return

> "While he was still a long way off, his father saw him... and ran to him." (Luke 15:20)

Meditation: The father didn't lecture or punish - he embraced. Patience makes space for others to grow and return on their own time.

Reflection: Can I wait with love for someone else to change?

Affirmation: "I choose love that doesn't rush healing."

4th Mystery: Jesus Waits Before Raising Lazarus

"When he heard that Lazarus was ill, he stayed two days longer..."(John 11:6)

Meditation: Jesus didn't rush. Sometimes delays are divine. Love isn't always urgent - sometimes it's about trusting the unseen.

Reflection: Do I believe something good is still coming, even when it's late?

Affirmation: "Love doesn't hurry. Love believes."

5th Mystery: Jesus Prays for Unity Among His Followers

"That they may all be one... as you, Father, are in me and I in you." (John 17:21)

Meditation: Understanding requires union - not sameness, but communion. It's not about winning arguments but seeing each other with grace.

Reflection: Can I choose connection over needing to be right?

Affirmation: "I seek to understand, not to control."

Closing Prayer

Our Lady of Compassion, hold my heart when I want to give up.

Teach me the patience of the Father, the slowness of Christ, and the understanding of those who listen with love.

Make me gentle with others and myself.

Let me grow in empathy and trust.

Amen.

Ancestral Healing

For those healing from generational pain, betrayal, abandonment, dysfunction, emotional neglect, or complicated ancestral ties. It's for the ones breaking cycles and still longing for love, safety, and home

Opening Prayer

O Lord, source of all healing and peace, we ask You to mend the bonds within our family.

Bring Your light to the wounds passed down through generations, and lift the burdens of pain and strife that weigh on our hearts.

Restore harmony where division lingers, and fill our lives with Your love and grace.

As we reflect and pray, guide us toward renewal and reconciliation, uniting us in the healing power of Your presence.

Amen.

1st Mystery: Joseph Is Betrayed by His Brothers

"They stripped him of his robe.. and sold him to the Ishmaelites for twenty pieces of silver." (Genesis 37:23-28)

Meditation: Family betrayal cuts deep. Joseph was rejected, thrown away by those who should have protected him but God was still writing his story. What others meant for harm, God turned into healing.

Reflection: Where have I been wounded by family - and how might God be writing redemption through it?

Affirmation: "Even betrayal cannot block my blessing."

2nd Mystery: Jesus Redefines Family

"Who are my mother and my brothers?'... 'Whoever does the will of God is my brother and sister and mother.'"" (Mark 3:33-35)

Meditation: Sometimes the family we're born into cannot love us well. Jesus shows us we're not bound by blood alone - we are free to choose a sacred family.

Reflection: Where do I need to redefine family for my healing?

Affirmation: "I am allowed to choose a safe, soul-aligned family."

3rd Mystery: Ruth Clings to Naomi

"Where you go I will go, and where you stay I will stay... your people will be my people."(Ruth 1:16)

Meditation: Not all families are tied by blood. Ruth lost everything - but she clung to the one who gave her love. In Naomi, she found chosen kinship and legacy.

Reflection: Who has stood by me with love - even when others didn't?

Affirmation: "I honor the ones who chose me. I am never alone."

4th Mystery: Jesus Heals the Boy with a Tormented Spirit

"From childhood it has thrown him into fire and water... But Jesus took him by the hand and lifted him to his feet."(Mark 9:21-27)

Meditation: Family wounds can begin in childhood - patterns passed down or inflicted early. But Jesus reaches into even long-held torment, and lifts us out with compassion.

Reflection: What childhood pain still needs the healing touch of Christ?

Affirmation: "No wound is too old for healing. I rise in love."

5th Mystery: Jesus on the Cross Gives Mary a New Son

"Woman, behold your son... Then he said to the disciple, 'Behold your mother.'" (John 19:26-27)

Meditation: Even as He died, Jesus tended to the emotional needs of His loved ones. He gave Mary and John to each other - a new family born in love and loss.

Reflection: What new relationships might God be inviting me to receive as a family?

Affirmation: "I am worthy of safe, healing love - even if it looks different."

Closing Prayer

You who know the ache of family sorrow, walk with me as I tend to these wounds.

Comfort me where love was absent.

Hold the parts of me that were never seen.

Guide me as I build something new- a family made of love, not fear.

If my family is toxic, may I find a new family in Christ, one filled with healing, understanding, and grace.

Help me to break and end any family curses, so that healing and peace may flow through generations to come. Amen.

Healing Sibling Rivalry

For those hurt by jealousy, comparison, competition, or distance between siblings

Opening Prayer

Virgin Mary, you raised Jesus alongside His kin with love, patience, and grace. Intercede for families suffering from division, especially among siblings.

Teach us how to love without comparison, and to forgive freely, as Jesus has loved us.

Amen.

1st Mystery: Cain and Abel

"Cain said to his brother Abel, 'Let us go out to the field.' And when they were in the field, Cain rose up against his brother Abel, and killed him... Then the Lord said, 'What have you done? Listen; your brother's blood is crying out to me from the ground!'" (Genesis 4:8-10)

Meditation: Imagine standing in the field where Cain and Abel's conflict took place. Hear the silence interrupted by violence, and feel the weight of jealousy and anger. Ask God to replace any seeds of envy in your heart with seeds of love and peace.

Reflection: Jealousy led Cain to violence. This ancient wound still echoes in families today. God sees the wounds that come from rivalry- and calls us to lay down anger, envy, and comparison, choosing love over resentment.

Affirmation: "I release envy and receive peace."

2nd Mystery: Joseph and His Brothers

> "Then Joseph said to his brothers, 'Come closer to me... I am your brother, Joseph, whom you sold into Egypt. And now do not be distressed, or angry with yourselves... for God sent me before you to preserve life.'"(Genesis 45:4-5)

Meditation: Picture Joseph standing before his brothers, the pain of betrayal still fresh, yet his heart full of forgiveness. Reflect on moments where you've been hurt-can you see God's hand bringing good even from those wounds?

Reflection: Joseph forgave those who deeply wronged him. Family healing takes time, but forgiveness opens the door to restoration. God can transform betrayal into blessing.

Affirmation: "With God's grace, I forgive and rebuild."

3rd Mystery: Miriam and Aaron's Jealousy of Moses

"Miriam and Aaron spoke against Moses... and they said, 'Has the Lord indeed spoken only through Moses? Has He not spoken through us also?' And the Lord heard it." (Numbers 12:1-2)

Meditation: Envision Miriam and Aaron, frustrated and comparing themselves to Moses. Think of your own gifts and roles in life. Take a moment to thank God for the unique purpose He has for you, without comparing it to others.

Reflection: Sometimes even spiritual gifts become sources of comparison. But God assigns unique roles to each soul. You don't need to compete for God's voice or favor— it is already yours.

Affirmation: "There is no competition in God's love."

4th Mystery: The Two Sons of the Prodigal Father

"Then he became angry and refused to go in. His father came out and began to plead with him... 'Son, you are always with me, and all that is mine is yours.'" (Luke 15:28-31)

Meditation: Picture the father pleading with the older son, his love for both children evident. Reflect on moments when you've felt resentment toward others' blessings. Pray for a heart that rejoices in God's generosity to all.

Reflection: The older brother struggled with resentment when his sibling was welcomed home. Jealousy can mask itself as fairness. But the Father loves each of His children fully, without withholding.

Affirmation: "God's love for others doesn't lessen His love for me."

5th Mystery: Jesus Restores Peter After Betrayal

> "Peter was grieved because He said to him the third time, 'Do you love me?' And he said, 'Lord, you know everything; you know that I love you.' Jesus said to him, 'Feed my sheep... What is that to you? Follow me!"(John 21:17-22)

Meditation: Imagine sitting beside Peter as Jesus restores him. Hear Jesus' gentle words and feel the call to follow Him without distraction. Consider areas in your life where you've compared yourself to others and let go of the need to compete.

Reflection: After being restored, Peter still looked over at John and compared their futures. Jesus lovingly redirected him: "What is that to you? Follow me." In the same way, we are called to follow Christ- not comparison.

Affirmation: "I follow Christ, not competition."

Closing Prayer

Jesus, Divine Brother, and Mary, our gentle Mother, bring peace into sibling relationships.

Help us to let go of old hurts and grow in mutual respect, healing, and love.

May every family divided by jealousy be reunited by grace.

Amen.

Black Sheep of the Family

For those who feel misunderstood, rejected, or unfairly treated by their family

Opening Prayer

Our Lady of Sorrows, who stood with love at the foot of the Cross, be with us as we lift up the wounds of rejection and misunderstanding.

Wrap us in your mantle, and help us see ourselves through your eyes and the eyes of your Son, Jesus, who was also rejected.

Amen.

1st Mystery: Joseph and the Coat of Many Colors

"Now Israel loved Joseph more than any other of his children... he made him a long robe with sleeves. But when his brothers saw that their father loved him more... they hated him, and could not speak peaceably to him."(Genesis 37:3-4)

Meditation: Close your eyes and imagine yourself in Joseph's place, wearing a coat that makes you stand out. Feel the weight of being both honored and resented. Breathe deeply, and let God remind you that His favor on your life is not diminished by others' opinions. Rest in the truth that you are chosen by Him.

Reflection: Joseph's favor from his father made him a target. Often, being "different" in a family invites jealousy, rejection, or misunderstanding. Yet Joseph's pain was the beginning of a divine purpose. You are not forgotten-you are chosen.

Affirmation: "God's favor is on me, even when others reject me."

2nd Mystery: David, the Forgotten Son

> "Jesse made seven of his sons pass before Samuel... And Samuel said to Jesse, 'Are all your sons here?' And he said, 'There remains yet the youngest, but he is keeping the sheep.'"(1 Samuel 16:10-13)

Meditation: Picture yourself as David, out in the fields, doing ordinary tasks while others are honored and seen. Hear the voice of God calling your name, reminding you that He sees what others overlook. Take a moment to feel His presence, choosing you for something greater.

Reflection: David was overlooked, uninvited to the gathering-but God saw him. If you feel invisible in your own family, remember that God exalts the unseen and anoints the overlooked.

Affirmation: "I am seen and chosen by God, even if others ignore me."

3rd Mystery: Jesus Rejected by His Own

> "He came to what was his own, and his own people did not accept him." (John 1:11)

Meditation: Imagine walking among people you know and love, only to be misunderstood or rejected. Now, picture Jesus walking beside you, sharing in your pain. Feel His compassion and understanding as He reminds you that He, too, was rejected, but overcame it for a greater purpose.

Reflection: Even Jesus experienced rejection from those closest to Him. If He was misunderstood, we can find comfort knowing we are not alone. You are in divine company.

Affirmation: "Jesus understands my pain, and walks with me through it."

4th Mystery: The Prodigal Son's Return

> "While he was still far off, his father saw him and was filled with compassion... 'This son of mine was dead and is alive again; he was lost and is found!'" (Luke 15:20-24)

Meditation: Picture yourself as the prodigal son, walking hesitantly toward home, unsure of what awaits. Now imagine the Father running toward you with arms wide open, filled with joy. Feel His embrace, His love, and His mercy, reminding you that no mistake is too big for His forgiveness.

Reflection: Sometimes being the "black sheep" comes with mistakes or separation. This mystery reminds us that God always runs to meet us with joy and mercy-no matter who has turned their back on us.

Affirmation: "God embraces me as His beloved child."

5th Mystery: Joseph Forgives His Brothers

> "Even though you intended to do harm to me, God intended it for good... So have no fear; I myself will provide for you and your little ones."(Genesis 50:20-21)

Meditation: Think of a time when someone hurt you deeply. Now, imagine releasing that pain to God, trusting Him to bring good out of the situation. Visualize yourself offering forgiveness, not to erase the pain, but to free your heart and allow God to work His purpose through you.

Reflection: Joseph chose forgiveness. Your story, too, is being woven for good. Forgiveness doesn't mean forgetting the pain, but it releases the weight to God.

Affirmation: "What was meant for harm, God is turning into purpose."

Closing Prayer

Mother Mary, Our Lady of Consolation, heal the heart of the one who feels cast aside.

Show them they are loved, chosen, and dignified.

May they be clothed in the Father's embrace and raised to walk in their divine identity.

Amen.

Conflict Resolution

For turning tension into transformation, argument into understanding, and relationships into sanctuaries of peace

Opening Prayer

Our Lady Queen of Peace, Our Lady of Mercy, and Our Lady of Reconciliation, I come before you seeking wisdom, grace, and mercy in the midst of conflict.

Teach me to approach tension with the Spirit's guidance, that I may bring peace where there is discord.

Amen.

1st Mystery: Cain and Abel

"Then the Lord said to Cain, 'Why are you angry?... If you do what is right, will you not be accepted?'"(Genesis 4:6-7)

Meditation: Jealousy and unspoken emotion festered into violence. God warned Cain, but he chose pride over peace. Conflict begins in the heart.

Reflection: What emotion am I avoiding or repressing that's fueling this conflict?

Affirmation: "I name what I feel with truth and tenderness."

2nd Mystery: Abigail Stops David from Revenge

> "David said... 'Blessed be your wisdom, and blessed be you, who have kept me from bloodshed today.'"(1 Samuel 25:32-33)

Meditation: Abigail's courage and wisdom stopped a king from making a deadly mistake. Sometimes, the person who brings peace is the one brave enough to speak up with love.

Reflection: Am I avoiding a hard conversation that could bring peace?

Affirmation: "I choose holy courage over silence or rage."

3rd Mystery: Jesus and the Woman Caught in Adultery

> ""Let the one among you who is without sin be the first to throw a stone.""(John 8:7)

Meditation: Conflict can lead to condemnation, but Jesus offers another path: self- reflection and mercy. The accusers left, and only grace remained.

Reflection: What stone do I need to drop before I speak?

Affirmation: "I choose mercy over judgment."

4th Mystery: Jesus Teaches to Reconcile Before the Altar

> "If you are offering your gift at the altar and remember your brother has something against you... first go and be reconciled."(Matthew 5:23-24)

Meditation: God desires peace between people before offerings. Sacred relationships come first. True worship includes reconciliation.

Reflection: Is there someone I need to forgive or ask forgiveness from?

Affirmation: "I seek healing before performance. Love first."

5th Mystery: Jesus Appears to His Disciples After Betrayal

> "Jesus came and stood among them and said, 'Peace be with you.'"(John 20:19)

Meditation: After abandonment and denial, Jesus could have scolded the disciples. But His first words were peace. Real peace often begins with grace that surprises.

Reflection: Am I willing to extend peace even before the apology?

Affirmation: "I sow peace where pain has been."

Closing Prayer

Our Lady Queen of Peace, teach me to breathe when I want to shout.

Teach me to listen when I want to defend. Teach me to bend without breaking. Let every conflict become an opportunity for healing.

Let my heart stay soft. Let my words be bridges. Let peace begin with me.

Amen.

Strained Relationships with Narcissistic Parents

For seeking grace and strength to remain compassionate, resilient, and centered in love amidst challenges

Opening Prayer

Our Lady of Compassion, Our Lady of Grace, and Our Lady of Resilience, I come before you in the midst of struggle, burdened yet hopeful.

Grant me the strength to maintain love in my heart, clarity in my thoughts, and gentleness in my actions as I face the difficulties of this relationship.

Guide me to respond with wisdom and grace, and remind me that I am worthy of dignity and respect.

Amen.

1st Mystery: Joseph and His Brothers

> "You intended to harm me, but God intended it for good to accomplish what is now being done, the saving of many lives." (Genesis 50:20)

Meditation: Betrayal and jealousy led Joseph's brothers to harm him, but God turned even this pain into a pathway of redemption. Joseph chose forgiveness, transforming bitterness into reconciliation.

Reflection: How can I release the weight of resentment, even when pain feels justified?

Affirmation: "I choose forgiveness, not for them, but to free myself from their hold over my heart."

2nd Mystery: Moses and the Israelites' Complaints

> "Moses also said, 'You will know that it was the Lord when He gives you meat to eat in the evening and all the bread you want in the morning... Who are we? You are not grumbling against us, but against the Lord.'" (Exodus 16:8)

Meditation: Moses endured ceaseless complaints and selfishness from the very people he led toward freedom. Yet, he stayed faithful, trusting God to guide him through their antagonism.

Reflection: How can I remain grounded in my values and trust God to sustain me in this challenging relationship?

Affirmation: "I look to God for strength and release the need for external validation."

3rd Mystery: Jesus Forgives Those Who Crucified Him

> "Jesus said, 'Father, forgive them, for they do not know what they are doing.'" (Luke 23:34)

Meditation: Even in His greatest suffering, Jesus forgave His persecutors, demonstrating that true strength lies in compassion. Forgiveness is not condoning wrongdoing but choosing not to be consumed by it.

Reflection: Am I able to separate the hurtful actions from the deeper wounds within my parent's heart?

Affirmation: "I release blame and create space for grace, even when forgiveness feels difficult."

4th Mystery: The Prodigal Son's Return

> "But while he was still a long way off, his father saw him and was filled with compassion for him; he ran to his son, threw his arms around him and kissed him."(Luke 15:20)

Meditation: The father in this parable displayed profound love and mercy, welcoming his wayward child with open arms. Even when we are hurt by someone, choosing compassion can begin the healing process.

Reflection: Can I balance healthy boundaries with a willingness to extend compassion when it is safe to do so?

Affirmation: "I preserve my boundaries while holding space for kindness and healing."

5th Mystery: Jesus Calms the Storm

"He got up, rebuked the wind and said to the waves, 'Quiet! Be still!' Then the wind died down and it was completely calm." (Mark 4:39)

Meditation: To follow Jesus is to trust His power to bring peace into the storms of our lives. Even amidst conflict, God offers calm and clarity to those who seek Him.

Reflection: How can I invite God's peace into moments of chaos or tension with my parent?

Affirmation: "I center myself in God's peace, allowing it to carry me through uncertainty."

Closing Prayer

Our Lady of Compassion, teach me to stand firm in my worth without harshness, to love without losing myself, and to forgive without compromising my boundaries.

Help me to see that even in struggle, I can find moments of grace. May my heart remain soft, my mind clear, and my spirit unshaken.

Guide me to peace, within myself and in this relationship.

Amen.

Healing from Sexual Abuse within the Family

For those carrying grief, confusion, and pain surrounding sexual abuse within or tolerated by family members

Opening Prayer

Mother Mary, Comfort of the Afflicted and Undoer of Knots, I come to you bearing deep wounds.

You who stood at the foot of the Cross and watched your Son suffer know what it is to witness evil and still carry light. I pray this rosary with you, for all survivors of sexual abuse within families.

May your Immaculate Heart be my refuge, and may your Son, the Divine Healer, restore what was broken. Let no shame remain, only truth, justice, and healing. Send the Holy Spirit to guide my heart and every person affected. In Jesus' name,

Amen.

1st Mystery: The Betrayal of Joseph by His Brothers

"They saw him from afar, and before he came near to them they conspired against him to kill him." (Genesis 37:18)

Meditation: Joseph was betrayed by those meant to protect him. Like many who suffer abuse in their families, his cries were not initially heard.

Reflection: You may feel alone and betrayed, but God never abandoned Joseph—and He has never abandoned you. God hears what others silence.

Affirmation: I am not what was done to me. God remembers me and is lifting me into justice and restoration.

2nd Mystery: Tamar and Her Brother Amnon

But he would not listen to her; and being stronger than she, he violated her and lay with her." (2 Samuel 13:14)

Meditation: Tamar's story is often left untold, but Scripture does not hide it. God sees every hidden abuse. He weeps with those who have been silenced and violated.

Reflection: God has never approved of what was done to you. He is the one who restores dignity when others have stolen it.

Affirmation: My voice matters. My story is sacred. God is a refuge for the violated.

3rd Mystery: Jesus Heals the Bleeding Woman

> "Daughter, your faith has made you well; go in peace, and be healed of your disease." (Mark 5:34)

Meditation: The woman reached for healing in a world that declared her unclean. In Jesus' eyes, she was always worthy.

Reflection: You are worthy of wholeness and love. Like her, you can reach for healing and find Jesus already reaching back.

Affirmation: I am loved, I am healing, and I am whole in the eyes of God.

4th Mystery: Jesus Weeps at the Tomb of Lazarus

> "Jesus wept." (John 11:35)

Meditation: Jesus weeps with the grieving. With the traumatized. With the abused. His tears mingle with yours.

Reflection: Your pain is not dismissed in Heaven. It is honored, it is witnessed, and it will be transfigured by Love.

Affirmation: Jesus weeps with me and walks with me into resurrection.

5th Mystery: Jesus Appears to Mary Magdalene After the Resurrection

"Jesus said to her, 'Mary.' She turned and said to him in Aramaic, 'Rabboni!'" (John 20:16)

Meditation: The risen Christ chose Mary Magdalene to receive the first Resurrection message—an outcast, a woman misunderstood.

Reflection: You, too, can rise. You are not forgotten. God is calling you by name into new life, new power, and new peace.

Affirmation: I am chosen. I rise. My healing is a testimony.

Closing Prayer

> Mother Mary, you who watched your child suffer, I entrust all wounded children and adults to your care.
>
> Help me reclaim my dignity, restore my voice, and walk boldly into healing.
>
> Banish the darkness of shame, and cover me in your mantle of light. Guide me to the resources, allies, and prayers that will support my journey.
>
> I surrender the pain to Christ's Sacred Heart and trust in His justice, mercy, and timing.
>
> Amen.

14

Rosaries for Romance

"Love is patient, love is kind. It does not envy, it does not boast, it is not proud." Corinthians 13:4

Romantic relationships bring love, companionship, and growth but can also present challenges. Dating requires self-awareness and trusting God to guide you toward the right partner. Long-distance and military couples face separation and uncertainty but can grow stronger through trust, communication, and faith. Healing from betrayal, breakups, or abuse is a journey of forgiveness and restoration, with God's grace offering clarity and renewal for broken hearts.

The following rosaries are designed to support you through these romantic journeys, whether you are building a healthy relationship, healing after heartbreak, or reclaiming peace after abuse. Through prayer, reflection, and divine guidance, may you find strength, clarity, and the courage to nurture love that mirrors God's unending kindness and compassion.

Healing After Separation or Divorce

For those who have loved and lost in marriage

Opening Prayer

> Mother Mary,
>
> You held the broken body of your Son in your arms — teach me to hold my own heart with tenderness.
>
> Intercede for me as I walk through the pain of separation.
>
> I bring to you every ache, every regret, every hope still flickering.
>
> Cover me in your mantle, hold me in your silence, and show me how to rise, not bitter — but more beautiful.
>
> Amen.

1st Mystery: The Breaking: When Love Fails

"Jesus wept." (John 11:35)

Meditation: Even Jesus cried when confronted with loss. There is no shame in tears. God is near to the brokenhearted.

Reflection: Sometimes things die that we thought would live forever — marriages, dreams, identities. This decade is for naming that death and grieving it honestly, without self-blame or bitterness.

Affirmation: "It is okay to feel this. God meets me in the sorrow."

2nd Mystery: The Loneliness: Facing the Empty Space

"It is not good for man to be alone." (Genesis 2:18)

Meditation: You were made for love and companionship. Feeling lonely now doesn't mean you failed — it means your heart is still open to connection.

Reflection: Even Jesus withdrew to lonely places to pray. In your solitude, you can hear God more clearly. Let this space become sacred.

Affirmation: "I am never truly alone. Divine love surrounds me."

3rd Mystery: The Reclaiming: Who Am I Now?

"Behold, I make all things new." (Revelation 21:5)

Meditation: The old identity may be gone — but your truest self remains untouched. Now begins the sacred work of rediscovering who you are in God.

Reflection: What if this loss is also a portal into wholeness? You are not half of something broken — you are a whole person becoming even more radiant.

Affirmation: "I am not what I lost. I am what is rising in me."

4th Mystery: The Forgiveness: Letting Go of Bitterness

> "Father, forgive them, for they know not what they do." (Luke 23:34)

Meditation: Forgiveness is not about condoning the harm. It's about freeing your own spirit from the shackles of resentment.

Reflection: Even Jesus, on the cross, extended forgiveness. Through Our Lady's intercession, let this decade become a softening of the heart — not for them, but for you.

Affirmation: "I forgive. Not because they deserve it — but because I deserve peace."

5th Mystery: The Hope: A New Future Is Possible

"Surely there is a future, and your hope will not be cut off." (Proverbs 23:18)

Meditation: This is not the end of your story. Love will come again — in new forms, with deeper wisdom.

Reflection: Let this final decade be a seed planted in hope. You may not see the blooms yet — but grace is already taking root.

Affirmation: "I trust in new beginnings. My story is still unfolding with beauty."

Closing Prayer

Sweet Mother Mary, comfort of the Afflicted and Mirror of Justice, you watched your Son be misunderstood, betrayed, and torn from the world.

Wrap me in your compassion.

Let my grief be an altar where transformation begins. I surrender this love that was, and open myself to the love that remains — divine, infinite, eternal.

Help me rise whole again.

Amen.

Becoming a Better Romantic Partner

For those seeking to cultivate love, empathy, and selflessness in their relationships

Opening Prayer

Heavenly Father, we come before You filled with hope and the desire to grow as loving and compassionate partners. Your love is the ultimate example of selflessness and care, and we long to reflect that in our relationships.

Guide us as we pray this Rosary for becoming a better romantic partner.

We ask for the intercession of the Blessed Virgin Mary, the pure model of tenderness and understanding, to inspire us to love with generosity, patience, and admiration.

Lord, teach us to listen, cherish, and honor our loved ones in ways that reflect Your divine goodness. May these prayers transform our hearts, deepening our capacity to love and serve selflessly.

Amen.

1st Mystery: Jesus Washes the Disciples' Feet

"Now that I, your Lord and Teacher, have washed your feet, you also should wash one another's feet. I have set you an example that you should do as I have done for you." (John 13:14-15)

Meditation: Jesus teaches us the true essence of love as selfless service. Being a good partner requires humility and a willingness to prioritize others' needs above our own, mirroring Christ's example of servant leadership.

Reflection: Do I actively look for ways to serve and support my partner, expecting nothing in return?

Affirmation: "I approach my relationship with humility, serving with Christ-like love."

2nd Mystery: The Good Samaritan

"But a Samaritan, as he traveled, came where the man was; and when he saw him, he took pity on him. He went to him and bandaged his wounds." (Luke 10:33-34)

Meditation: Love calls us to respond with empathy and care. A good partner learns to share in their loved one's joys and burdens, offering kindness and support during both good times and struggles.

Reflection: Am I compassionate and attentive enough to truly understand the feelings and needs of my partner?

Affirmation: "I grow in empathy and nurture our bond through care and understanding."

3rd Mystery: The Feeding of the Five Thousand

"Taking the five loaves and the two fish, and looking up to heaven, He gave thanks and broke the loaves. Then He gave them to the disciples, and the disciples gave them to the people... They all ate and were satisfied." (Matthew 14:19-20)

Meditation: Jesus shows us the power of gratitude and generosity. A loving relationship flourishes when we regularly express gratitude for our partner and share our time, affection, and affirmations freely.

Reflection: Do I take time to show appreciation for my partner, no matter how small the gesture?

Affirmation: "I am thankful for my partner and cherish them with heartfelt gratitude."

4th Mystery: The Wedding at Cana

""They have no more wine,' Jesus' mother said to Him. His mother said to the servants, 'Do whatever He tells you.'" (John 2:1-3)

Meditation: At the wedding in Cana, Jesus blessed the couple and performed His first miracle through love and trust. A strong partnership relies on a foundation of mutual trust, faith, and admiration for the unique beauty of one another.

Reflection: Do I openly admire and affirm the beauty, talents, and goodness of my partner, lifting them up with words and actions?

Affirmation: "I admire and affirm my partner, cherishing them as God's gift."

5th Mystery: The Beatitudes

> "Blessed are the meek, for they will inherit the earth... Blessed are the merciful, for they will be shown mercy... Blessed are the pure in heart, for they will see God." (Matthew 5:3-12)

Meditation: The Beatitudes remind us of the virtues that lead to joyful and healthy relationships. By striving for meekness, kindness, and purity of heart, we can foster love and harmony in our partnership.

Reflection: Am I striving to grow in virtuous behavior, always wanting the best for my partner and our relationship?

Affirmation: "I embody humility, kindness, and love, desiring joy for my partner."

Closing Prayer

Blessed Mother, perfect model of love and devotion, pray for us as we seek to embody God's love in our relationships.

Help us to listen with patience, understand with compassion, and love with hearts full of grace and admiration.

May our relationships reflect God's goodness and become a source of joy and strength.

Guide us to become better partners, always seeking to lift each other toward Christ.

Amen.

Long-Distance or Military Couples

For those experiencing distance within their relationship

Opening Prayer

Our Lady of the Way,

You journey with those who are apart, whose hearts ache with longing.

I come to you now, asking for your guidance and protection. Help us to trust that love is stronger than distance, and that every separation holds the promise of reunion. Be our anchor, our guide, and our hope.

Amen.

1st Mystery - Ruth's Loyalty to Naomi

"Where you go I will go... Your people will be my people, and your God my God."(Ruth 1:16-17)

Meditation: Ruth's love transcended separation - a vow of loyalty that changed destinies.

Reflection: Can I trust that love is stronger than distance?

Affirmation: "Though miles apart, our hearts remain aligned."

2nd Mystery - The Centurion's Faith for a Distant Healing

> "Only say the word, and my servant will be healed... and his servant was healed at that moment."(Matthew 8:8,13)

Meditation: Love doesn't require physical presence to be powerful. The centurion trusted in the unseen, and so can we.

Reflection: Am I nurturing this relationship with prayer as much as presence?

Affirmation: "Distance is not a barrier to love or miracles."

3rd Mystery - Paul Writes Letters from Prison

> "I thank my God every time I remember you... because of your partnership in the Gospel." (Philippians 1:3-5)

Meditation: Paul's letters became vessels of connection and grace, proving that words and prayers hold immense power.

Reflection: How can I be intentional about communicating my love?

Affirmation: "Every message I send can carry grace."

4th Mystery - Mary Waits for Jesus

"His mother treasured all these things in her heart." (Luke 2:51)

Meditation: Mary waited with faith and love through silence and absence, holding space for what was to come.

Reflection: What am I being invited to treasure in this time apart?

Affirmation: "My waiting is sacred. I am still growing in love."

5th Mystery - Jesus Promises to Prepare a Place

"I go to prepare a place for you... and I will come back and take you to be with me." (John 14:2-3)

Meditation: Even Jesus spoke words of reunion, reminding us that every goodbye holds the promise of return.

Reflection: What kind of reunion am I dreaming of and praying for?

Affirmation: "This absence will not last forever. Love will reunite us."

Closing Prayer

Our Lady of the Way, travel with our hearts when we cannot travel with our bodies.

Guard our bond from fear, distraction, and doubt.

Help us grow in trust, deepen our communication, and believe in reunion.

Be our anchor, our map, and our guide.

Keep our love holy across all distances.

Amen.

Healing After a Breakup

For those who are navigating the pain of breaking up, whether needing to leave a relationship or healing from recent heart-break

Opening Prayer

Mother Mary, Comforter of the Afflicted,

I come to you in my sorrow and confusion. Help me to entrust my broken heart to your care and the care of your Son, Jesus.

Guide me toward peace, clarity, and healing as I walk this path. Help me to remember that my worth is found in the love of God, who will never abandon me.

Amen.

1st Mystery: Jesus in the Garden of Gethsemane

"Then he said to them, 'I am deeply grieved, even to death; remain here, and stay awake with me.' And going a little farther, he threw himself on the ground and prayed, 'My Father, if it is possible, let this cup pass from me; yet not what I want but what you want.'" (Matthew 26:38-39)

Meditation: Imagine yourself in the garden with Jesus, feeling the weight of heartbreak and uncertainty. Jesus understands the pain of letting go, of surrendering what is safe and familiar for what is right and necessary. Rest in the knowledge that He is with you in this anguish, and He will strengthen you.

Reflection: Even in His sorrow, Jesus chose to trust the Father's plan. Breaking away from a relationship can feel like losing a piece of yourself. Yet in surrender, there is hope for renewal and healing. God's plan for your life remains good, even in this season of heartache.

Affirmation: "God is with me in the pain, and His plan for me is good."

2nd Mystery: Jesus Encounters the Samaritan Woman at the Well

"Jesus said to her, 'Everyone who drinks of this water will be thirsty again, but those who drink of the water that I will give them will never be thirsty. The water that I will give will become in them a spring of water gushing up to eternal life.'"(John 4:13-14)

Meditation: Picture yourself sitting by a well, weary and longing for answers. Jesus sits beside you, His eyes filled with understanding and compassion. He offers you water that quenches far more than physical thirst-it refreshes your very soul. Accept His invitation to find fulfillment in Him alone.

Reflection: When relationships end, it's natural to feel an emptiness inside. Yet Jesus reminds us that only His love can truly satisfy the deepest longings of our hearts. Take this time to lean on Him, and trust that His love is enough.

Affirmation: "Only Jesus can fill the deepest places in my heart."

3rd Mystery: Jesus Heals the Brokenhearted

"The Lord is near to the brokenhearted and saves the crushed in spirit."(Psalm 34:18)

Meditation: Envision Jesus sitting beside you as you share the pain of your breakup with Him. Feel His presence as He gently binds your wounds and reminds you that He is close to you at this moment. He whispers words of hope and reminds you of your priceless worth.

Reflection: Heartbreak feels like a fracture in the soul, but the Lord is near, offering comfort and healing. Though the current pain feels overwhelming, this moment is not the end of your story. Trust in His ability to restore your heart.

Affirmation: "God is near to me and is healing my heart."

4th Mystery: The Hope of God's Plans

> "For surely I know the plans I have for you, says the Lord, plans for your welfare and not for harm, to give you a future with hope." (Jeremiah 29:11)

Meditation: Imagine your heart as a garden, tenderly cared for by a loving gardener. Though some branches are pruned away, trust that God is nurturing the soil for new growth. Lift your heart to Him and invite His hope to take root.

Reflection: A breakup can feel like a loss of all plans and dreams for the future. But God reminds us that His plans are always for good, full of promise and renewal. Trust that He is preparing you for a bright future.

Affirmation: "God is creating new plans and hope for my future."

5th Mystery: The Promise of New Beginnings

"Do not remember the former things, or consider the things of old. I am about to do a new thing; now it springs forth, do you not perceive it?"(Isaiah 43:18-19)

Meditation: Picture a barren field as rain begins to fall, turning dry soil into new life. Allow yourself to release the past and open your heart to the fresh work God is doing in your life. Feel the hope of new beginnings taking hold within you.

Reflection: Breaking away from a relationship can grieve the heart, but it is also an opportunity for a new chapter. God makes all things new, and He is faithful to bring beauty from ashes. Trust Him with what is ahead and find joy in the promise of renewal.

Affirmation: "God is making a new path for me, and I will walk forward in hope."

Closing Prayer

Holy Spirit, guide my steps as I move forward from this season of heartbreak. Fill me with your peace and remind me that I am deeply loved, seen, and valued by God.

Help me to trust in the plans You have for me, and to walk each day in the assurance of Your presence. Mother Mary, intercede for me as I seek healing and wholeness.

Amen.

Abusive Relationships

For those who endure abuse in their partnerships, seeking strength, protection, and healing

Opening Prayer

Holy Mary, Comforter of the Afflicted, intercede for those suffering in abusive relationships.

Wrap them in your compassionate mantle, and grant them the courage to seek safety and healing. O Lord, shield your children from harm, renew their strength, and remind them of their worth and dignity in your sight.

Amen.

1st Mystery: Hagar's Escape into the Wilderness

"The angel of the Lord found her by a spring of water in the wilderness... He said, 'Hagar, where have you come from and where are you going?"(Genesis 16:7-8)

Meditation: Picture yourself in Hagar's place, fleeing into an uncertain wilderness to escape mistreatment. Remember that God sent His angel to meet her in her darkest moment, offering guidance and reassurance. Take a deep breath, and hear God asking you, "Where have you come from, and where are you going?" Trust that He meets you where you are and guides your next steps.

Reflection: Hagar felt alone and abandoned, yet she encountered God's presence in her isolation. If you are feeling trapped or lost, remember that God sees you and calls you by name. He remains with you as you seek shelter and deliverance from harm.

Affirmation: "God sees me, hears me, and provides for me in my time of need."

2nd Mystery: The Woman Caught in Adultery

> "Jesus straightened up and said to her, 'Woman, where are they? Has no one condemned you?' She said, 'No one, sir.' And Jesus said, 'Neither do I condemn you. Go your way, and from now on do not sin again.'"(John 8:10-11)

Meditation: Imagine Jesus looking at you with complete compassion, defending you from accusations of shame or guilt. Feel His gentle yet firm call to rise above your situation and move forward in grace. You are not defined by others' judgments or actions against you; you are defined by God's unending love and mercy.

Reflection: Jesus offered protection and restoration, even to those most vulnerable and condemned. Whether the abuse you face is verbal, physical, or emotional, He stands ready to shield you and offers you a path of healing and renewal.

Affirmation: "Jesus protects me and restores my dignity."

3rd Mystery: The Samaritan Woman at the Well

"Jesus said to her, 'Everyone who drinks of this water will be thirsty again, but those who drink of the water that I will give them will never be thirsty.'"(John 4:13-14)

Meditation: Picture yourself sitting at the well, weary and burdened from your struggles. Jesus approaches and offers you living water-peace, strength, and healing that no one can take away. Breathe deeply, and accept His gift of renewal and life abundant.

Reflection: The Samaritan woman faced rejection and shame in her community, yet Jesus sought her out personally. Like her, you are not beyond His reach or love. He sees your pain and offers a healing that runs deeper than any wound inflicted by others.

Affirmation: "I accept the living water Christ gives; my soul is restored."

4th Mystery: Jesus Calms the Storm

"Jesus woke up and rebuked the wind, and said to the sea, 'Peace! Be still!' Then the wind ceased, and there was dead calm. He said to them, 'Why are you afraid? Have you still no faith?'"(Mark 4:39-40)

Meditation: Imagine yourself in a boat battered by waves, feeling overwhelmed and afraid, but see Jesus standing and calming the storm. Feel His peace wash over you, silencing the chaos. Know that even in the stormiest moments of your life, He holds the power to bring calm and safety.

Reflection: Life with an abusive partner can feel like being caught in an unrelenting storm. Trust that Jesus is in the boat with you, ready to still the tempest and guide you to safety when you call on Him.

Affirmation: "Jesus brings peace to the storms in my life and leads me to safety."

5th Mystery: The Resurrection of Jesus

"Why do you look for the living among the dead? He is not here, but has risen."(Luke 24:5-6)

Meditation: Visualize yourself standing before the empty tomb, experiencing the hope that comes with the resurrection. Remember that resurrection follows suffering, and God's power to bring life from death is at work in your life. Trust Him to lead you out of darkness into the light of renewal and hope.

Reflection: Just as Christ triumphed over death, you too are called to rise above the pain and suffering, stepping into a new life of freedom and peace. Abundant life is possible when we place ourselves in God's hands and trust in His plan.

Affirmation: "I have hope in Christ's resurrection; new life awaits me beyond this pain."

Closing Prayer

Most Holy Mother, Queen of Peace, intercede for those enduring abuse.

Teach them to seek help, courage, and healing in their daily struggles.

Father God, may your infinite mercy and love be their refuge, and may the Holy Spirit guide them into paths of peace, freedom, and restoration.

Wrap them in your divine protection.

Amen.

Healing After Betrayal or Distance

For those aching in the aftermath of broken trust - whether that betrayal was physical, emotional, or even spiritual

Opening Prayer

O Mary, Our Lady of Sorrows and Our Lady of Mercy, we turn to you in our grief and brokenness, bringing before you the wounds of betrayal and distance.

You who know the deepest sorrows, intercede for us and bring comfort to our aching hearts.

Guide us through the shadows of pain and help us take steps toward healing and renewal. May your tender presence bring us peace and strength.

Amen.

1st Mystery: Judas Betrays Jesus with a Kiss

"Judas... approached Jesus to kiss him. But Jesus asked him, Judas, are you betraying the Son of Man with a kiss?"" (Luke 22:47-48)

Meditation: Some wounds come from those we've loved most. Betrayal stings deeper when it's disguised as love. Jesus felt it, named it, and did not harden.

Reflection: Where have I been wounded by someone I trusted?

Affirmation: "Even in betrayal, I am still held by God."

2nd Mystery: Peter Denies Jesus Three Times

"The Lord turned and looked at Peter... and he went outside and wept bitterly." (Luke 22:61-62)

Meditation: Peter didn't mean to betray Jesus - but fear won. In relationships, sometimes people fail us not from malice, but weakness. Jesus looked at Peter with sorrow, not hatred.

Reflection: Is there someone who has failed me but also grieves it?

Affirmation: "I release bitterness and make room for honest grief."

3rd Mystery: The Risen Jesus Appears to the Disciples

"Jesus came and stood among them and said, 'Peace be with you.'" (John 20:19)

Meditation: After abandonment, Jesus offers peace. He doesn't shame or scold, he breathes peace into the ones who left Him. This is divine reconciliation.

Reflection: Am I ready to receive peace, even if the wound is still tender?

Affirmation: "Peace is my inheritance - I allow it in."

4th Mystery: Jesus Reinstates Peter

"Jesus said, 'Do you love me?'... And He said, 'Feed my sheep.'" (John 21:17)

Meditation: Jesus doesn't just forgive Peter He gives him a purpose. Reconciliation is not just about fixing the past - it's about empowering the future.

Reflection: If healing is possible, what would reconciliation look like?

Affirmation: "Love is stronger than shame. Purpose can rise from pain."

5th Mystery: The Prodigal Son Returns

"While he was still a long way off, his father saw him and was filled with compassion." (Luke 15:20)

Meditation: This mystery reminds us that coming back - to self, to God, or to one another begins with mercy. The father runs, embraces, and restores.

Reflection: Do I need to return to someone - or allow them to return to me?

Affirmation: "Mercy is always moving toward me."

Closing Prayer

> Our Lady of the Wounded Heart, you know the ache of broken trust.
>
> You stayed at the foot of the Cross, watching love suffer - and still, you believed in resurrection.
>
> Teach me how to heal.
>
> Teach me how to forgive or how to lovingly let go.
>
> Hold my heart in this rebuilding. Let love rise again.
>
> Amen.

Shared Purpose and Mission in Love

For couples who want their relationship to be about more than romance - about service, legacy, and spiritual partnership, for those called to build, heal, serve, or create together with God as their center

Opening Prayer

Heavenly Father, we come before You as a couple, united in love and guided by Your divine purpose. Thank You for the gift of partnership, for calling us to walk this path together with You at our center.

We seek Your guidance as we commit to a relationship rooted in service, legacy, and spiritual partnership. Help us to be instruments of Your healing, builders of Your kingdom, and a reflection of Your love in all that we do.

May our hearts be aligned with Your will, and may we walk together in unity and agreement, as Your Word declares in Amos 3:3. We pray with the intercession of Our Lady of Unity, Our Lady Seat of Wisdom, and Our Lady of Apostles, trusting that their prayers will sustain us in our shared mission.

Amen.

1st Mystery: Adam and Eve Are Given the Garden

"The Lord God took the man and put him in the Garden... It is not good for man to be alone; I will make a helper suitable for him."(Genesis 2:15-18)

Meditation: Their first calling wasn't just to love each other - but to tend to something together. All true love includes sacred work.

Reflection: What "garden" are we being invited to steward together?

Affirmation: "We are partners in purpose, not just romance."

2nd Mystery: Priscilla and Aquila Serve Together

"They explained the way of God more accurately..."(Acts 18:2-3, 26)

Meditation: This married couple was known for teaching, discipline, and opening their home to the early Church. Their relationship was a vessel of ministry.

Reflection: How are we using our gifts to bless others as a couple?

Affirmation: "Our love is a light for others, not just ourselves."

3rd Mystery: Mary and Joseph Raise the Christ Together

"The child grew and became strong... and the grace of God was on Him."(Luke 2:39-40)

Meditation: Mary and Joseph's shared mission wasn't glamorous - but it was holy. They parented with purpose, raising love incarnate with protection, humility, and faith.

Reflection: What are we nurturing together that carries divine purpose?

Affirmation: "We protect and grow what God has entrusted to us."

4th Mystery: Jesus Sends the Disciples Out Two by Two

"Calling the Twelve to Him, He began to send them out two by two..."(Mark 6:7)

Meditation: Even Jesus didn't send people out alone. He knew the strength in mutual witness. Purpose is more sustainable when shared with someone you trust.

Reflection: What mission could we step into more fully if we walked it together?

Affirmation: "Together, we go further and deeper in God's call."

5th Mystery: Jesus Prays for Unity in Love

"That they may all be one, as you, Father, are in me and I in you..."(John 17:21)

Meditation: Jesus prayed for divine oneness - a love so rooted in God that it mirrors the Trinity. That is the sacred union we are called to live and reflect.

Reflection: Is our union helping us become more like Christ?

Affirmation: "Our love reflects divine unity and brings heaven closer to earth."

Closing Prayer

Our Lady of Unity,

Make our love fruitful, not just romantic.

Show us how to build together -to co-create a life that serves others, honors God, and leaves beauty behind.

Bless our calling, our timing, and our teamwork.

Where one is weak, let the other rise.

Where one dreams, let the other plant.

Make us a holy pair —rooted in mission, rich in love.

Amen.

Engaged and Newlywed Couples

For couples wanting to begin their covenant with intention, prayerfulness, and grace

Opening Prayer

Heavenly Father, we come before You with grateful hearts, asking Your blessing on all engaged and married couples.

May their unions be rooted in Your love, guided by Your grace, and strengthened by faith. Grant them wisdom, patience, and enduring love as they walk this sacred path together.

Through the intercession of the Blessed Virgin Mary, may they always keep You at the center of their lives.

Amen.

1st Mystery: Mary and Joseph Journey Together to Bethlehem

"Joseph went up from Nazareth... with Mary, who was pledged to be married to him and was expecting a child."(Luke 2:4-5)

Meditation: The first days of their marriage were marked by discomfort, travel, and uncertainty - yet Mary and Joseph walked together, united in mission.

Reflection: Can I embrace discomfort as part of our shared beginning?

Affirmation: "We walk this path together, with grace and trust."

2nd Mystery: The Wedding at Cana

"When the wine ran short... His mother said to the servers, 'Do whatever He tells you.'"(John 2:1-5)

Meditation: Even joyful unions will face moments of lack. But when God is invited, lack becomes transformation. Mary intercedes, and Jesus blesses.

Reflection: Where can I invite God to renew or multiply joy in our relationship?

Affirmation: "God is invited into our love. Miracles will come."

3rd Mystery: The Holy Family Flees to Egypt

"Take the child and his mother and flee.. for Herod is going to search for the child to kill him."(Matthew 2:13-15)

Meditation: The first year of family life required protection, sacrifice, and courage. Marriage is not just celebration - it's choosing each other in hardship too.

Reflection: How can we protect and prioritize each other in a world of noise?

Affirmation: "We are each other's safe place."

4th Mystery: Jesus Washes the Feet of His Disciples

> "I have set you an example that you should do as I have done for you."(John 13:14-15)

Meditation: Marriage thrives when love is rooted in service. This mystery invites both partners to kneel — not in weakness, but in humility and strength.

Reflection: Where can I serve my partner with more joy and tenderness?

Affirmation: "Love is service, not scorekeeping."

5th Mystery: The Disciples on the Road to Emmaus

> "Jesus himself drew near and walked with them, but their eyes were kept from recognizing him."(Luke 24:15-16)

Meditation: Sometimes, the divine presence in our relationships isn't obvious. But when we walk together, even through grief or confusion, Jesus walks beside us.

Reflection: Are we making space for the sacred in our shared journey?

Affirmation: "Christ walks with us, even in silence."

Closing Prayer

> Our Lady,
>
> Bless our beginning. teach us to cherish each other, to laugh, to grow, to yield, and to build our foundation on your Son.
>
> May our love reflect heaven, and our home be a sanctuary of peace.
>
> Protect our vows. deepen our joy.
>
> Amen

Being Violated on a Date

For those healing from dating abuse or date rape

Opening Prayer

Mother Mary, Our Lady of Sorrows, you held your broken son in your arms and did not turn away. You saw his suffering and never once blamed him. I ask you to see me now with that same gaze of love and protection.

Wrap your mantle around me. Intercede for me. Walk with me through this prayer, as I offer each bead to reclaim my story, restore my spirit, and remind myself that I am not alone.

Let each Hail Mary be a healing balm. Let each mystery bring me closer to peace.

St. Raphael, angel of healing. St. Dymphna, patron of mental health. St. Maria Goretti, who chose purity even in pain. Be near to me now.

Amen

1st Mystery: The Annunciation – Consent Matters

"Let it be done to me according to your word." (Luke 1:38)

Meditation: Mary's "yes" was freely given. God waited for her consent. Even Heaven honors free will.

Reflection: Abuse steals consent. It crosses sacred boundaries. God never forces, manipulates, or violates. When others do, they are acting against God, not for Him.

Affirmation: I reclaim the power of my "yes" and my "no." My body is sacred. God protects my freedom and my dignity.

2nd Mystery: The Agony in the Garden – When Fear Paralyzes

"My soul is sorrowful unto death... Yet not my will, but Yours be done." (Matthew 26:38–39)

Meditation: Jesus felt terrified and overwhelmed. He asked friends to stay awake with Him, but they didn't. He understands what it's like to feel abandoned in your most vulnerable hour.

Reflection: You are not weak for freezing. You are not guilty for being afraid. You are a survivor. Jesus was there.

Affirmation: Even in fear, I was not forsaken. My body's response was wise. I survived, and I am healing.

3rd Mystery: The Crowning with Thorns – Humiliation and Shame

> "They stripped Him and put a scarlet robe on Him... and mocked Him." (Matthew 27:28–29)

Meditation: Jesus endured public humiliation and mockery. He was shamed and violated by those who should have protected Him.

Reflection: Shame is a lie. You did nothing wrong. God does not mock or shame you. He comforts the humiliated.

Affirmation: I release the shame that was never mine to carry. I wear the crown of dignity God has placed upon me.

Fourth Mystery: The Crucifixion – Bearing the Pain

> "They crucified Him... but standing by the cross was His mother." (John 19:18,25)

Meditation: Pain is real. Trauma wounds deeply. But even at the Cross, Mary stood close. God does not run from your pain—He meets you in it.

Reflection: You are not defined by what happened to you. Healing is possible. God is not afraid of your wounds.

Affirmation: I am not what was done to me. I am beloved, held, and healing. Mary stands beside me.

Fifth Mystery: The Resurrection – Reclaiming Life

"Why do you look for the living among the dead? He is not here—He is risen." (Luke 24:5–6)

Meditation: Jesus rose in glory. His wounds became part of His story—but they did not define His future.

Reflection: You can rise too. Your story is not over. The light is already breaking through. Your healing matters.

Affirmation: I choose life. I rise with Christ. My healing begins anew today.

Closing Prayer

Mother Mary, walk with me in my healing. Undo every knot of fear, shame, and self-blame.

Help me reclaim my body, my voice, and my worth. Let me feel safe again in my skin.

Protect me from any who would cause harm. Intercede for my healing and renew my strength. Let this rosary be the beginning of peace, power, and love.

Amen.

Discernment in Dating

For those in the dating or relationship-discernment phase-calling on the Holy Spirit for clarity, self-worth, and divine timing

Opening Prayer

Heavenly Father,

We come before You with open hearts, seeking Your guidance and wisdom as we navigate the path of love and relationships. Through the intercession of Our Lady of Good Counsel, grant us clarity in our decisions.

With Our Lady of the Way, lead us along the path You have planned for us.

And through Our Lady Undoer of Knots, help us untangle the doubts, fears, and insecurities that weigh us down. Holy Spirit, fill us with trust in Your divine timing, remind us of our inherent worth, and guide us to align our hearts with Your will.

As we pray this rosary, may we grow in faith, patience, and love, trusting that You are working all things for our good.

Amen.

1st Mystery: Rebekah Meets Isaac

"Let the one whom You have chosen for your servant Isaac... be the one who offers water to me and my camels." (Genesis 24:14-19)

Meditation: Abraham's servant prayed for signs of character - kindness, generosity, service - not appearance. And God responded. Discernment begins with surrendering the search to divine wisdom.

Reflection: Am I looking for a partner through ego or through spirit?

Affirmation: "I trust God to reveal what's real."

2nd Mystery: David and Michal's Misalignment

"Michal... despised him in her heart."(2 Samuel 6:20-23)

Meditation: They loved each other once-but weren't aligned in their purpose. David danced before the Lord with passion; Michal was embarrassed. Sacred alignment is key.

Reflection: Are our hearts dancing toward the same spiritual direction?

Affirmation: "I choose alignment over attachment."

3rd Mystery: Jesus and the Samaritan Woman at the Well

"'You are right... the man you now have is not your husband.'"(John 4:17-18)

Meditation: Jesus saw her truth and freed her from shame. Discernment includes naming patterns that no longer serve. Her transformation began with honesty.

Reflection: What relational pattern am I being invited to heal?

Affirmation: "I let go of false loves to receive true love."

4th Mystery: Mary Says Yes to God's Plan

"I am the handmaid of the Lord. Let it be done to me according to your word." (Luke 1:38)

Meditation: Mary didn't chase or force love-she said yes to the divine plan. When dating, surrender doesn't mean passivity. It means trusting that divine timing brings divine partnership.

Reflection: Am I forcing a story, or listening for the divine script?

Affirmation: "I trust love to find me at the right time."

5th Mystery: Jesus Chooses His Disciples with Prayer

"Jesus went out to the mountain to pray, and spent the night in prayer... then He chose twelve."(Luke 6:12-13)

Meditation: Before choosing intimate relationships, Jesus retreated and prayed. Discernment must be spiritual - not just romantic or emotional.

Reflection: Have I prayed more than I've texted or swiped?

Affirmation: "I choose sacred love through prayerful discernment."

Closing Prayer

Our Lady of Good Counsel,

I surrender my search for love to You.

Let me not settle out of fear or loneliness.

Help me notice the red flags, trust divine timing, And honor my own worth.

Guide me to love that mirrors Your Son - steady, wise, faithful, and kind.

Amen.

Sacred Union

For couples seeking a deeper spiritual, emotional, and mystical bond of love

Opening Prayer

Holy Mother, Queen of Heaven,

We come before you with humility and devotion to honor the sacred gift of love you have given us.

Guide us with your wisdom as we strive to live out God's call to partnership — a union rooted in trust, faith, and selfless love.

Through your intercession, may our love reflect the peace of Christ's teachings, drawing us closer to Him.

Strengthen our bond, inspire virtue, and lead us to unity with the Divine Will. Blessed Mother, grant us grace, balance, and the blessings of everlasting love.

Amen.

1st Mystery: Adam and Eve Walk with God in the Garden

"The man and his wife were both naked, and they felt no shame... and they heard the sound of the Lord God walking in the garden." (Genesis 2:25; 3:8)

Meditation: Sacred union begins in Eden - a place of openness and walking with God. Returning to union means walking together in divine intimacy, without hiding.

Reflection: Where am I invited to be more emotionally or spiritually vulnerable with my partner?

Affirmation: "In God's presence, our union becomes holy ground."

2nd Mystery: Jacob and Rachel's Longing

> "So Jacob served seven years to get Rachel, but they seemed like only a few days to him because of his love for her." (Genesis 29:20)

Meditation: True union is marked by patience and dedication. Time becomes sacred when love is the reason for the effort.

Reflection: Do I see my partner as a divine gift worth tending to with care?

Affirmation: "I love patiently, and I honor the wait."

3rd Mystery: The Wedding at Cana

> "Jesus and his disciples had also been invited to the wedding... and the wine ran Out." (John 2:1-11)

Meditation: Even in sacred unions, the wine sometimes runs out. But Mary sees the need, and Jesus renews the joy. Love invites God to transform moments of lack into abundance.

Reflection: Where in my relationship do I need God to renew joy and hope?

Affirmation: "God turns ordinary love into miracle wine."

4th Mystery: Mary and Joseph's Pilgrimage

> "Every year they went to Jerusalem for the Festival... but the boy Jesus stayed behind... they began looking for him." (Luke 2:41-45)

Meditation: Sacred union doesn't guarantee ease. Mary and Joseph faced fear and confusion but searched together. They stayed united in difficult moments.

Reflection: In the hard times, do I seek answers with my partner or try to face challenges.alone?

Affirmation: "We walk together, even when the path is unclear."

5th Mystery: Christ and the Church as Bride and Bridegroom

> "This is a profound mystery-but I am talking about Christ and the Church." (Ephesians 5:31-32)

Meditation: Marriage is an icon of the eternal covenant between Christ and His Church. Our unions are meant to reflect the divine love that binds us to God.

Reflection: How can my relationship more fully reflect God's love and truth?

Affirmation: "We are a living sacrament of divine love."

Closing Prayer

Our Lady of Divine Love,

Bless this union.

May it be a place of healing, joy, and prayer.

Teach us to walk together in Eden and wilderness, to labor with joy like Jacob, to celebrate like Cana,

To search like Mary and Joseph, and to love like Christ and His Church.

Amen.

Trust in Love

For individuals and couples to deepen faith, release fear, and co-create loving, secure relationships with God at the center

Opening Prayer

Heavenly Father,

We come before You with open hearts, longing for Your perfect love to fill us. Thank You for the gift of love, which reflects Your divine nature. We seek to deepen our faith in You, releasing all fear and doubt.

As we pray this Rosary of Trust in Love, we ask for the intercession of:

- Our Lady of Confidence, to boldly trust in Your providence.

- Our Lady of Perpetual Help, to find strength in our trials.

- Our Lady of Hope, to remain steadfast in Your promises.

Surround us with Your grace and guide us in creating loving, secure relationships with You at the center. May Your perfect love cast out all fear, and may we grow in unity and peace.

Amen.

1st Mystery: Joseph Decides to Stay with Mary

> "Joseph... did not want to expose her to public disgrace... but after he had considered this, an angel appeared... 'Do not be afraid to take Mary as your Wife.'" (Matthew 1:19-24)

Meditation: Joseph's love was tested. Instead of abandoning Mary in fear or pride, he trusted God's plan and stayed-faithfully, silently, and courageously.

Reflection: Where am I being invited to trust instead of walk away?

Affirmation: "I choose love even when it feels uncertain."

2nd Mystery: Ruth Chooses to Stay with Naomi

> "Where you go I will go, and where you stay I will stay. Your people will be my people."(Ruth 1:16)

Meditation: Ruth shows covenant love a choice to remain, even when logic says leave. Trust in relationships often begins with choosing to stay present.

Reflection: Am I present in love, or only when it's easy?

Affirmation: "I remain rooted in love through devotion and presence."

3rd Mystery: Jesus Calms the Storm

"He rebuked the wind... 'Peace! Be still!' Then He asked them, 'Why are you so afraid? Do you still have no faith?" (Mark 4:39-40)

Meditation: Storms challenge relationships. Jesus teaches us that peace comes not from calm waters, but from trust in the One who is always with us.

Reflection: Do I trust the relationship more than the emotions of the moment?

Affirmation: "God is with us in the storm. I choose peace."

4th Mystery: The Woman with the Hemorrhage Reaches Out

""Daughter, your faith has made you well. Go in peace and be freed from your suffering.""(Mark 5:34)

Meditation: She reached out in vulnerability and found healing. Love often requires the courage to admit what hurts and ask for help.

Reflection: What wound do I need to expose to bring healing to my relationship?

Affirmation: "Vulnerability is strength. Love can heal me."

5th Mystery: Jesus Washes the Disciples' Feet

"Now that I... have washed your feet, you also should wash one another's feet." (John 13:14-15)

Meditation: Trust is built through small, humble acts of love. Service, not control, creates safety and strengthens relationships.

Reflection: How can I love more humbly in this relationship?

Affirmation: "I build trust through humility, kindness, and care."

Closing Prayer

Our Lady of Confidence,

Hold our love when we are afraid.

Teach us to trust each other not through perfection, but through faith, forgiveness, and courage.

Show us that real love is not about control, but about presence, patience, and peace.

May our love reflect the trust of Joseph, the loyalty of Ruth, and the faith of those who reach for healing.

Amen.

15

Rosaries for Spiritual Growth and Inner Peace

"Trust in the Lord with all your heart, and lean not on your own understanding; in all your ways submit to Him, and He will make your paths straight." - Proverbs 3:5-6

Life often presents us with challenges that can stir negative emotions like anger, impatience, and selfishness. These emotions can block us from experiencing the grace and peace that are our birthright. Proverbs reminds us to trust in God's wisdom and submit to Him, allowing Him to guide our paths. By incorporating the rosary into daily practice, you can work through these difficult emotions, finding healing and transformation in the process.

The following rosaries are designed to help you navigate challenging emotions and grow spiritually. By praying them, you can begin to find hope, patience, and the inner peace needed to overcome struggles.

Peace in Anxiety

For finding calm when the heart is heavy, the future feels uncertain, or the mind won't stop racing

Opening Prayer

> Our Lady, Mirror of Calm, walk with me. Lord, bring stillness to my heart and mind.
>
> May Your peace fill the spaces where fear and uncertainty dwell.
>
> Amen.

1st Mystery: Jesus Calms the Storm

"Then he got up, rebuked the winds and the sea, and there was a great calm." (Matthew 8:26)

Meditation: Jesus calms the raging storm with just a word. Though the waves crash and the boat rocks, He remains still-inviting us to trust Him.

Reflection: Anxiety often feels like being tossed at sea. But even the storm knows His voice. No wave is louder than His Word.

Affirmation: I trust that God's voice is stronger than the chaos of my fears.

2nd Mystery: The Angel Strengthens Jesus in Gethsemane

"Then an angel from heaven appeared to him and gave him strength." (Luke 22:43)

Meditation: Even in His anguish, Jesus did not suffer alone-help was sent. God provided the strength He needed to face the cross.

Reflection: Anxiety isolates us, but God sends comfort in many forms: whispers, people, moments of stillness. We are never abandoned.

Affirmation: I am never alone; God's strength and comfort are always near.

3rd Mystery: Mary Hears Simeon's Prophecy

"And a sword will pierce your own soul too."(Luke 2:35)

Meditation: Mary receives the prophecy of suffering to come. She does not run from it but holds it in her heart with grace and trust.

Reflection: Anxiety often comes from fearing "what if." Mary shows us how to carry unknown futures without losing peace.

Affirmation: I can face the unknown with grace and trust, knowing God is with me.

4th Mystery: Jesus Appears in the Upper Room

"Peace be with you." (John 20:19)

Meditation: The Risen Christ enters the locked room where His friends hid in fear and breathes peace over them. His presence brings comfort, not condemnation.

Reflection: No locked door-no panicked mind-can keep Jesus out. He comes not to scold but to bring peace.

Affirmation: Christ's peace is greater than my fears, and He meets me where I am.

5th Mystery: The Woman with the Flow is Healed

"Daughter, your faith has healed you. Go in peace and be free from your suffering." (Mark 5:34)

Meditation: The woman reaches out in faith despite her fear and exhaustion. Her quiet courage brings her the healing she longed for.

Reflection: Anxiety drains us, but even small acts of faith-like reaching for Him-can bring renewal. Sometimes, just touching grace is enough.

Affirmation: Even in my weakness, my faith connects me to God's healing grace.

Closing Prayer

Our Lady, Mirror of Calm, pray for me.

Lord, help me trust Your voice over the noise of my fears. May Your peace fill my heart and guide my steps.

Amen.

Brokenhearted

For those grieving the loss of someone or something deeply loved

Opening Prayer

> Our Lady of Sorrows, walk with me.
>
> Lord, You are close to the brokenhearted. Hold my grief gently in Your hands and help me see Your presence in my pain.
>
> Amen.

1st Mystery: Jesus Weeps at Lazarus' Tomb

> "Jesus wept. Then the Jews said, 'See how he loved him!'" (John 11:35-36)

Meditation: Even Jesus wept. He didn't avoid His grief but embraced it. His love and loss. were intertwined.

Reflection: What part of my heart needs permission to grieve fully?

Affirmation: My grief is sacred. God weeps with me.

2nd Mystery: Mary Stands at the Foot of the Cross

"Standing by the cross of Jesus were his mother... Jesus said, 'Woman, behold your son." (John 19:25-27)

Meditation: Mary didn't turn away from suffering. She stayed, even with a shattered heart, trusting in God's plan.

Reflection: Am I willing to stay present with my pain instead of pushing it away?

Affirmation: I can face my sorrow. Mary stands with me.

3rd Mystery: The Garden of Gethsemane

"And being in anguish, he prayed more earnestly, and his sweat was like drops of blood." (Luke 22:44)

Meditation: Grief often feels isolating. Jesus understands this. He surrendered His pain to God and received strength to carry on.

Reflection: What part of my sorrow do I need to place into God's hands today?

Affirmation: Even in anguish, I am held.

4th Mystery: The Road to Emmaus

"Jesus himself came near and went with them, but their eyes were kept from recognizing him."(Luke 24:15-16)

Meditation: Grief can cloud our vision. Even when we don't see Him, God walks with us through every step of the journey.

Reflection: Where have I missed the presence of God in my grief?

Affirmation: Even when I can't see Him, Jesus walks with me.

5th Mystery: He Will Wipe Away Every Tear

"He will wipe every tear from their eyes. There will be no more death or mourning or crying or pain..."(Revelation 21:4)

Meditation: Grief is not the end. Resurrection is real, and one day our tears will be transformed into joy.

Reflection: What hope can I hold onto, even as I grieve?

Affirmation: My pain will not have the final word.

Closing Prayer

Our Lady of Sorrows, Mother who knows grief, hold me as I mourn.

Let my tears fall freely, and let me find Jesus beside me in my pain. Teach me that resurrection always follows the cross.

Amen.

Healing Anger

For those seeking to transform anger into peace and grace

Opening Prayer

Heavenly Father, we come to You carrying the weight of anger, frustration, and bitterness.

You are the source of all peace and healing, and we long to bring our emotions into alignment with Your will.

Guide us as we pray this Rosary for Healing Anger.

We ask for the intercession of Our Lady, Queen of Peace, to walk with us on this journey, bringing calm to our hearts and clarity to our actions.

May we honor our emotions while allowing Your grace to transform them into something holy.

Amen.

1st Mystery: Cain and Abel - Anger Without Accountability

"Then the Lord said to Cain, 'Why are you angry?... Sin is crouching at your door; it desires to have you, but you must rule over it." (Genesis 4:6-7)

Meditation: God didn't shame Cain for his anger but warned him to master it. Anger becomes dangerous when we let it drive us without reflection.

Reflection: Where am I letting anger rule instead of reveal?

Affirmation: "I feel my anger, but it does not control me."

2nd Mystery: Moses Strikes the Rock

"Moses struck the rock twice with his staff... but the Lord said, 'You did not trust in me enough to honor me as holy.'" (Numbers 20:10-12)

Meditation: Moses was faithful, but in his frustration, he acted out of impulse, not obedience. Even righteous anger can block blessings when misused.

Reflection: Have I struck when I should've spoken?

Affirmation: "I respond with wisdom, not reaction."

3rd Mystery: Jesus Flips the Tables in the Temple

"Jesus entered the temple... and overturned the tables... 'My house shall be a house of prayer!'" (Matthew 21:12-13)

Meditation: Not all anger is wrong. Jesus demonstrates righteous anger-focused on injustice, not people; guided by purpose, not ego.

Reflection: Where can I channel my anger into sacred action?

Affirmation: "My anger can become fuel for justice, not destruction."

4th Mystery: Jonah's Bitterness is Met with Compassion

> "But the Lord said, 'Is it right for you to be angry?'" (Jonah 4:4)

Meditation: Jonah was angry that God forgave others. God didn't shame him but invited reflection. Anger often masks deeper pain, grief, or fear.

Reflection: What deeper wound might my anger be protecting?

Affirmation: "I explore the pain beneath my rage with grace."

5th Mystery: Jesus Breathes Peace Over Fear and Shame

> "Peace be with you... As the Father has sent me, I am sending you." (John 20:19-21)

Meditation: The disciples were hiding, possibly in fear or anger at themselves. Jesus entered with peace, not judgment. Peace is where transformation begins.

Reflection: Am I willing to let peace in, even when I feel unworthy of it?

Affirmation: "I choose peace. I open my heart to calm and clarity."

Closing Prayer

> Mother Mary, Queen of Peace, receive the fire in my chest.
>
> Help me to feel anger without harming others. Let my rage transform, not destroy. May my emotions serve healing and justice, not ego.
>
> Jesus, Prince of Peace, reign in my mind and heart, granting me calm and clarity in every day.
>
> Amen.

Patience and Trust in Divine Timing

For surrender, faith, and peace in waiting

Opening Prayer

Mary, Mother Most Patient,

You waited in faith for your Son to come into the world and trusted God's plan even when it seemed delayed or unclear.

Teach me to rest in the slow unfolding of divine timing.

Intercede for me, that I may receive the grace of holy patience and be still, knowing God is working all things for good.

Amen.

1st Mystery: Abraham's Long Wait for the Promise

"Then the word of the Lord came to him: 'This man will not be your heir; but a son who is your own flesh and blood will be your heir.'"(Genesis 15:4)

Meditation: God promised Abraham a son, but it took years to fulfill. Trusting God means surrendering our timelines. Patience is not passive-it's faithful waiting.

Reflection: Where do I need to let go of control and trust God's timing in my life?

Affirmation: "God is never late. He is preparing something holy."

2nd Mystery: Joseph in Prison Before His Rise

> "The Lord was with Joseph and showed him steadfast love."(Genesis 39:21)

Meditation: Joseph faced betrayal, slavery, and imprisonment before his dreams came true. Delays are often part of God's preparation for something greater.

Reflection: Can I trust that God is working in my waiting, even when I don't see it?

Affirmation: "Even in darkness, God is working my deliverance."

3rd Mystery: The Israelites in the Desert

> "The Lord your God has led you these forty years in the wilderness."(Deuteronomy 8:2)

Meditation: God used the Israelites' time in the wilderness to humble and teach them. Delays often prepare us to receive the promise.

Reflection: How is God using this season of waiting to develop my character?

Affirmation: "The wilderness is not wasted-it's preparation."

4th Mystery: Mary's Hidden Years

"Mary treasured up all these things and pondered them in her heart."(Luke 2:19)

Meditation: Mary trusted God's plan, even when she didn't fully understand it. Patience often requires silent trust and holy pondering.

Reflection: Can I trust God to work in the silence and the waiting?

Affirmation: "I trust what God conceives in silence will bear fruit."

5th Mystery: Jesus Delays but Comes

"Lord, if You had been here, my brother would not have died..."(John 11:21)

Meditation: Jesus delayed going to Lazarus, yet His timing revealed God's glory. Divine delay is often divine design.

Reflection: Do I believe that God's timing always brings about the greatest good?

Affirmation: "Jesus is never late. He is coming with power."

Closing Prayer

O Mary, Queen of Patience and Mother of Divine Timing,

Thank you for teaching me to trust God even when His plans seem hidden.

Help me not to rush ahead in fear or frustration. Make me still. Make me faithful.

Make me willing to wait in love and move in obedience.

I surrender time itself to the Lord of Eternity.

Amen.

Fighting Obtrusive Thoughts

For reclaiming peace, rejecting lies, and resting in truth

Opening Prayer

Mother Mary,

Queen of Peace,

Wrap my thoughts in your mantle.

Jesus, speak truth into the echoes of fear.

Holy Spirit, flood me with calm and clarity.

I renounce what is not of God, and I claim my peace.

Amen.

1st Mystery: Jesus Resists the Devil in the Wilderness

"Then Jesus was led by the Spirit into the wilderness to be tempted... 'Away from me, Satan! For it is written...'" (Matthew 4:1-11)

Meditation: Even Jesus was attacked by lies. The devil whispered: prove yourself, turn stone to bread, jump, bow down. Jesus didn't argue - He answered with truth.

Reflection: What lie keeps repeating in my mind, and what truth can replace it?

Affirmation: "I speak truth to the lies. I am not what I fear."

2nd Mystery: Elijah Hears God in the Whisper

"After the fire came a gentle whisper... and Elijah wrapped his face in his cloak."(1 Kings 19:11-13)

Meditation: Overwhelmed and depressed, Elijah fled into the wilderness. God didn't show up in drama or fire - He whispered. Elijah listened and rested.

Reflection: Am I willing to quiet the noise and tune into the whisper of God's peace?

Affirmation: "God speaks gently. I choose stillness over panic."

3rd Mystery: The Man with Legion is Set Free

"My name is Legion," he replied, "for we are many."... And the people saw him sitting, clothed, and in his right mind. (Mark 5:1-15)

Meditation: Tormented by a thousand voices, the man was freed when Jesus spoke peace. Demons screamed; Jesus silenced them. The man sat still, whole again.

Reflection: What needs to be cast out of my mind today in Jesus' name?

Affirmation: "No voice is louder than my healing. My mind is returning to peace."

4th Mystery: Paul Takes Every Thought Captive

> "We take captive every thought to make it obedient to Christ."(2 Corinthians 10:3-5)

Meditation: The battle isn't just in the world - it's in the mind. But we are not powerless. Take that thought. Bind it. Rewire it. Replace it with truth.

Reflection: Which thoughts today need to be taken captive and released?

Affirmation: "I have authority. My mind is not a battlefield - it is sacred ground."

5th Mystery: Mary Magnifies the Lord

> "My soul magnifies the Lord... for He has looked upon His lowly servant." (Luke 1:46-49)

Meditation: Mary didn't spiral — she magnified. To magnify is to make bigger. She could've focused on fear, but instead she focused on divine goodness.

Reflection: What am I magnifying - fear or faith?

Affirmation: "My soul magnifies peace. I shift the lens."

Closing Prayer

> Mother Mary,
>
> Cover my mind with your protective mantle.
>
> Crush the serpent of evil thoughts that seeks to cloud my heart and soul.
>
> Jesus, speak truth to the lies and fears that echo within me.
>
> Holy Spirit, pour your calm and clarity over me.
>
> I renounce all that is not of God, and I claim the peace that comes from your Son.
>
> Under your guidance, Mother, I find rest and protection.
>
> Amen.

Embracing Your Spiritual Role

For accepting your calling, celebrating others' gifts, and finding peace in your unique place in God's plan

Opening Prayer

O Lord, help me accept the mission You've assigned to me. May I find peace in my position, joy in others' victories, and strength to carry the gifts You've entrusted to me.

Through the intercession of Our Lady, the Seat of Wisdom, and the guidance of Mary Magdalene, may I walk in divine confidence.

Amen.

1st Mystery: Mary Magdalene is Called to Witness

"Jesus said to her, 'Mary.' She turned and said to him in Aramaic, 'Rabboni!' (which means Teacher). Jesus said, 'Do not hold on to me, for I have not yet ascended to the Father. Go to my brothers and say to them..'" (John 20:16-17)

Meditation: Mary Magdalene was chosen to witness the Resurrection-an honor none of the male disciples received. This sacred duty may have incited confusion or jealousy, but she answered it faithfully.

Reflection: How do I respond when God calls me to a task that others might not understand or support?

Affirmation: "I will answer God's call with courage, even when others don't affirm it."

2nd Mystery: The Disciples Argue About Rank

> "An argument arose among them as to which of them was the greatest. But Jesus... said to them, 'Let the greatest among you become as the youngest, and the leader as one who serves." (Luke 22:24-26)

Meditation: The disciples, though close to Jesus, struggled with jealousy. Christ's correction reminds us that true greatness lies in service, not comparison.

Reflection: In what ways do I compare myself to others instead of celebrating their service?

Affirmation: "I choose humility and service over competition and envy."

3rd Mystery: Paul Affirms the Many Roles in the Body of Christ

"The body does not consist of one member but of many... If the whole body were an eye, where would be the sense of hearing?" (1 Corinthians 12:14,17)

Meditation: Paul reminds us that we each have different but essential roles in the Church. Envy of another's gifts diminishes our own.

Reflection: Am I trying to fulfill someone else's calling instead of honoring my own?

Affirmation: "My role in God's plan is holy, needed, and sacred."

4th Mystery: Jesus Rebukes Exclusive Spiritual Judgment

"John said, 'Master, we saw someone driving out demons in your name and we tried to stop him, because he is not one of us.' Jesus replied, 'Do not stop him... whoever is not against you is for you.'" (Luke 9:49-50)

Meditation: Even the apostles wanted to exclude others who weren't "in the circle." But Jesus affirmed the legitimacy of spiritual work outside their control.

Reflection: Do I believe only certain people are qualified to do God's work?

Affirmation: "God works through whomever He chooses, even those I don't expect."

5th Mystery: Mary Magdalene's Boldness in the Gospel of Mary

"Peter said to Mary, 'Sister, we know the Savior loved you more than the rest of women. Tell us the words of the Savior which you remember.' Mary answered and said, 'I will tell you what is hidden from you." (Gospel of Mary, 5:2-3)

Meditation: Mary stood her ground despite the disciples' doubts and discomfort. She shared her vision faithfully, even though it was met with resistance.

Reflection: Am I hiding my gifts or truths out of fear of rejection?

Affirmation: "I will boldly share the insights God gives me, even when others question my worth."

Closing Prayer

Mary, humble handmaid and exalted Queen of Heaven, pray for us to accept our divine assignments with love and clarity.

May we not covet another's calling but rejoice in the mission entrusted to us. Help us embrace our place in the Body of Christ with courage and peace.

Amen.

Discernment and Choosing the Light

For vigilance, wisdom, and walking in the Divine Light

Opening Prayer

O Most Holy Virgin, Our Lady of Discernment and Radiant Light, guide us as we pray.

Enoch walked with God, and we too desire to walk in holiness, discerning truth from illusion, obedience from rebellion.

Help us recognize the tempter's subtle snares, and anchor our hearts in the Divine Will.

Amen.

1st Mystery: The Fall of the Watchers

"And the angels, the children of heaven, saw and lusted after them.. and they taught them charms and enchantments, and the cutting of roots, and made them acquainted with plants."(1 Enoch 7:1-2, 8:1)

Meditation: The Watchers were once holy but fell through temptation. Discernment begins with guarding the eyes and the heart.

Reflection: Where have I allowed curiosity or cravings to lead me astray?

Affirmation: "I choose wisdom over impulse. I guard my senses and walk in truth."

2nd Mystery: The Corruption of Knowledge

> "And Azazel taught men to make swords and knives and shields... and there arose much godlessness, and they committed fornication, and they were led astray and became corrupt in all their ways."(1 Enoch 8:1-2)

Meditation: Knowledge without Divine guidance can lead to harm. Discernment is knowing when wisdom becomes dangerous.

Reflection: Do I use knowledge and skills to glorify God or for personal gain?

Affirmation: "I walk in holy wisdom. I use my gifts to serve the Light."

3rd Mystery: Enoch Walks with God

> "And Enoch walked with God: and he was not; for God took him." (Genesis 5:24)

Meditation: Enoch lived in obedience and intimacy with God, becoming a vessel for heavenly visions.

Reflection: Do I spend time walking with God daily, even in silence?

Affirmation: "I walk in step with the Divine. My life is a prayer unfolding."

4th Mystery: The Vision of the Coming Judgment

> "Behold, He comes with ten thousands of His holy ones to execute judgment... to convict all the ungodly of their deeds."(1 Enoch 1:9)

Meditation: God's justice is perfect, even when it feels delayed. Discernment is trusting in Divine timing.

Reflection: Do I try to control outcomes or trust God's justice and mercy?

Affirmation: "I trust the Lord's justice. I act with integrity and leave judgment to God."

5th Mystery: The Eternal Light of the Righteous

> "The elect shall dwell in light, joy, and peace, and they shall inherit the earth... and their faces shall shine with joy." (1 Enoch 58:3, 62:15)

Meditation: Walking in the Light leads to joy and eternal peace.

Reflection: Do I trust that the path of holiness holds more joy than the shadows ever could?

Affirmation: "I am called to joy. I choose the Light, and the Light chooses me."

Closing Prayer

O Blessed Mother, Our Lady of Discernment, wrap us in your veil of wisdom.

Help us reject what glitters but is false, and walk bravely in the fire of truth.

May the example of Enoch, and your constant maternal intercession, keep us steady until we shine with the joy of the elect.

Amen.

Beginning New Chapters

For crossing into new beginnings, spiritual transitions, and walking boldly into God's promises

Opening Prayer

Mother Mary, Gate of Heaven and Keeper of Thresholds,

I offer you this prayer as I prepare to cross into the new.

Wrap me in your mantle as I leave behind what no longer serves. may I enter with clarity, peace, and purpose.

Let no fear remain, only trust and sacred guidance.

Amen.

1st Mystery: The Israelites Cross the Red Sea

> "Then Moses stretched out his hand over the sea, and the Lord drove the sea back... The people of Israel went into the midst of the sea on dry ground." (Exodus 14:21-22)

Meditation: Crossing the Red Sea symbolizes the moment we leave bondage behind and walk in faith toward freedom.

Reflection: What old fear or attachment am I being called to leave behind?

Affirmation: "I walk forward in faith. The waters will part before me."

2nd Mystery: Ruth Crosses into Bethlehem

> "Where you go, I will go; where you stay, I will stay. Your people will be my people and your God my God."(Ruth 1:16)

Meditation: Ruth left all she knew to follow the Spirit into the unknown. She walked through grief and found grace.

Reflection: Where am I being asked to follow trustfully, even if the road ahead is uncertain?

Affirmation: "I do not walk alone. Grace goes before me."

3rd Mystery: Mary Enters Elizabeth's Home

> "And she entered the house of Zechariah and greeted Elizabeth. When Elizabeth heard Mary's greeting, the child leaped in her womb.."(Luke 1:40-41)

Meditation: Mary crossed a threshold of service and connection. In doing so, she awakened joy in others.

Reflection: What relationships or sacred spaces am I being asked to bless by showing up?

Affirmation: "My presence brings holy joy."

4th Mystery: Jesus is Baptized in the Jordan

> "Jesus came up out of the water... and behold, a voice from heaven said, 'This is my beloved Son, with whom I am well pleased.'" (Matthew 3:16-17)

Meditation: Baptism marks the start of divine mission. Jesus crossed from hidden life into public purpose.

Reflection: What calling is waiting for me on the other side of surrender?

Affirmation: "I am ready to live my calling. Heaven is pleased with me."

5th Mystery: The Women Discover the Empty Tomb

> "Why do you seek the living among the dead? He is not here, but has risen." (Luke 24:5-6)

Meditation: This is the ultimate threshold - from death to life, grief to glory. The tomb is empty.

Reflection: What old belief, grief, or identity is ready to be laid to rest?

Affirmation: "I rise into new life. Resurrection lives in me."

Closing Prayer

> Thank you, Mary,
>
> Gate of the Dawn, Keeper of Thresholds,
>
> For walking with me from one chapter to the next.
>
> May I enter this new beginning with faith, and leave fear behind at the door.
>
> Let my steps be blessed, and my heart always open to the call.
>
> Amen.

Fasting and Physical Discipline

For honoring your body as a temple and aligning your hunger with divine grace

Opening Prayer

Beloved Mother Mary, Mediatrix of Grace,

Guide me as I offer my body, my hunger, and my cravings to God.

Let this fast be about devotion, not denial.

Help me detach from distractions and cling to what nourishes my soul.

May this fast be a holy offering, united with your Son's sacrifice.

Amen.

1st Mystery: Jesus Fasts in the Wilderness

> "After fasting forty days and forty nights, he was hungry." (Matthew 4:2)

Meditation: Jesus enters the wilderness, hungry but full of purpose. His hunger becomes holy-fuel for strength and discernment.

Reflection: What "wilderness" am I in right now? What temptations arise when I feel hunger-physical or spiritual?

Affirmation: "With Christ, my hunger becomes sacred. I am strengthened in stillness."

2nd Mystery: The Hidden Fast of Mary

"But Mary treasured all these things and pondered them in her heart." (Luke 2:19)

Meditation: Mary's life was a quiet offering, filled with hidden sacrifices of time, comfort, and expectation.

Reflection: How can I imitate Mary's inner fast-letting go of pride, urgency, or control?

Affirmation: "I fast not only with my body, but with my heart. I choose silence, simplicity, and trust."

3rd Mystery: Jesus Feeds the 5,000

"Then Jesus took the loaves, gave thanks, and distributed to those who were seated as much as they wanted." (John 6:11)

Meditation: Hunger and surrender lead to abundance. Jesus multiplies what little is offered.

Reflection: When I crave food or comfort, can I surrender my hunger to Jesus, trusting in spiritual abundance?

Affirmation: "I trust in divine nourishment. Even in lack, I have all that I need."

4th Mystery: Jesus' Agony in the Garden

> "Being in anguish, he prayed more earnestly, and his sweat was like drops of blood." (Luke 22:44)

Meditation: Fasting is surrender. Jesus, in his weakest moment, gave his ultimate "yes" to God.

Reflection: When this fast feels hard, can I unite my struggle with Christ's sacrifice?

Affirmation: "I am never alone in sacrifice. My surrender is holy."

5th Mystery: The Resurrection of the Body

> "He who raised Christ from the dead will also give life to your mortal bodies." (Romans 8:11)

Meditation: Fasting isn't about perfection but transformation. God desires our healing and wholeness.

Reflection: What new life is emerging as I release old habits or cravings?

Affirmation: "I am being renewed. My body is a vessel of light and purpose."

Closing Prayer

Mother Mary,

Wrap me in your mantle of grace as I walk the path of physical discipline.

May my fast bring healing, not harm-strength, not shame.

Help me honor the temple God gave me.

Let my every craving be an invitation to pray,

And my hunger be a reminder to feed my soul.

Amen.

Connect to the Angels

For those wanting angelic messages and angelic protection

Opening Prayer

Queen of Angels, beloved Mother Mary,

You who guide the hosts of heaven with gentle love, help me open my heart to the whispers of the angels.

May I recognize their presence, receive their messages with clarity, and find refuge in the protection they offer.

Wrap me in your mantle of grace, and lead me closer to your Son, through the ministry of the angels you reign over.

Amen.

1st Mystery: Mary's Fiat

"Behold, I am the handmaid of the Lord; may it be done to me according to your Word." (Luke 1:38)

Meditation: At the Annunciation, Mary's yes to God not only welcomed salvation but also embraced the message delivered by the angel

Gabriel. Her openness to the angelic message shows us how to receive divine guidance with humility and faith.

Reflection: How can I open my heart to recognize and receive the messages God sends through His angels, trusting their guidance in my life?

Affirmation: "With Mary's fiat as my guide, I open my heart to receive and follow the messages of God's angels."

2nd Mystery: The Angel's Message to Joseph

> "But after he had considered this, an angel of the Lord appeared to him in a dream and said, 'Joseph son of David, do not be afraid to take Mary home as your wife, because what is conceived in her is from the Holy Spirit. She will give birth to a son, and you are to give him the name Jesus, because he will save his people from their sins."(Matthew 1:20-21)

Meditation: The angel's message to Joseph revealed God's plan and reassured him to trust in His will. Joseph's obedience, even in uncertainty, reminds us of the courage needed to follow God's path.

Reflection: Do I trust in God's guidance, even when it challenges my understanding? How can I respond with faith and courage to His call in my life?

Affirmation: "I trust in God's plan, knowing that His guidance leads me to fulfill His purpose."

3rd Mystery: Joseph is Warned by an Angel to Protect Jesus

"An angel of the Lord appeared to Joseph in a dream. 'Get up,' he said, 'take the child and his mother and escape to Egypt. Stay there until I tell you, for Herod is going to search for the child to kill him.'" (Matthew 2:13)

Meditation: God sent an angel to guide Joseph, protecting the Holy Family from danger. Through Joseph's obedience, Jesus and Mary were kept safe, showing us the importance of trusting divine guidance.

Reflection: How can I remain attentive to God's guidance in protecting those I love?

Affirmation: "I trust in God's guidance and follow His will to protect those entrusted to my care."

4th Mystery: The Angels Minister to Jesus

"Then the devil left him, and behold, angels came and ministered to him." (Matthew 4:11)

Meditation: After Jesus was tempted in the wilderness, angels brought Him comfort and strength. Their presence reminds us of God's care and the support we receive through heavenly messengers.

Reflection: When I feel weary or burdened, can I trust the angels to bring me comfort and encouragement?

Affirmation: "I am never alone; the angels sustain me in my trials."

5th Mystery: Mary's Coronation as Queen of Angels

> "A great sign appeared in the sky, a woman clothed with the sun, with the moon under her feet, and on her head a crown of twelve stars." (Revelation 12:1)

Meditation: Mary is crowned as Queen of Heaven and Earth, reigning with her Son and directing the angels in their missions. Her coronation signifies the ultimate victory of God's grace and the closeness of heaven to earth.

Reflection: How can I honor Mary as Queen of Angels and call upon her intercession to connect with their guidance?

Affirmation: "I rejoice in the Queen of Angels, whose love bridges heaven and earth."

Closing Prayer

Queen of Angels,

Through your intercession, may I grow in trust and connection with the heavenly messengers.

Guide me to hear their wisdom and feel their protection each day.

Help me to love as you love, serve as you served, and walk alongside the angels.

Wrap me in your mantle of light and peace, that I may live under the constant care of your angelic kingdom.

Amen.

Appendix: FAQs About the Rosary

The Rosary is a powerful and transformative prayer, but it is also surrounded by questions and misconceptions. This section addresses some of the most common questions about the Rosary, offering clarity and guidance for those seeking to deepen their practice.

1. Is the Rosary Used in Exorcisms?

Yes, the Rosary is often used in exorcisms as a sacred tool of prayer and protection. However, it is important to understand that the Rosary itself is not a talisman or magical object. Its power doesn't solely lie in the physical beads but in the prayers and faith of the person using it. When prayed with devotion, the Rosary invites Mary's intercession and creates an environment of divine presence that evil cannot endure.

The repetitive prayers of the Rosary, especially the Hail Mary, invoke Mary's purity and obedience, which stand in direct opposition to the rebellion and corruption of demonic forces. It is a reminder that the Rosary is a spiritual weapon, not a charm, and its effectiveness depends on the faith and intention of the one praying.

2. Will the Rosary Automatically Grant My Every Request?

No, the Rosary is not a tool for selfish wish fulfillment. While Mary has promised graces and blessings to those who devoutly pray the

Rosary, it is not a guarantee that every request will be granted in the way you expect. The Rosary is a prayer of trust and surrender, inviting you to align your will with God's plan.

Through the Rosary, you may find that your desires and priorities shift, and you begin to see God's hand at work in your life in unexpected ways. It is a prayer that transforms the heart, helping you to trust in God's timing and wisdom.

3. How Will the Rosary Bring Grace and Change Into My Life?

Praying the Rosary daily is a practice of opening your heart to God's grace. Over time, you may notice subtle but profound changes in your life:

- A greater sense of peace and clarity.
- Increased patience and compassion.
- A deeper connection to Mary and her maternal care.
- A growing desire to live a life aligned with God's will.

However, the Rosary also has a way of revealing areas of your life that need healing or change. If you are holding onto *sin or resisting God's grace, you may find it difficult to maintain a daily practice of praying the Rosary. This is not a failure but an invitation to reflect on what is holding you back and to ask for Mary's help in overcoming it.

(*Sin, according to Catholic teaching, is defined as an offense against God and a failure to love Him and others as we are called to. It is a deliberate choice to turn away from God's law, disrupting our relationship with Him and often with those around us. The Catechism of the Catholic Church describes sin as "an utterance, a deed, or a desire contrary to the eternal law" (CCC 1849).

On a deeper, more spiritual level, sin can also be understood as that which creates resistance in our lives—resistance to love, to grace, and to becoming the fullest version of ourselves in alignment with God's will. It is anything that keeps us trapped in patterns of selfishness, fear, or pride, preventing us from fully experiencing the love of God and sharing that love with others. Sin erects barriers within us, reducing our capacity to give and receive love freely, and calls us to seek healing and forgiveness through grace.)0

4. Can the Rosary Spark an Interest in Abrahamic Ideologies and Other Biblical Teachings?

Yes, praying the Rosary often sparks a deeper interest in other aspects of faith, such as scripture, saints, angels, demonology, etc. As you meditate on the mysteries of the Rosary, you may feel drawn to learn more about the lives of Jesus and Mary, the stories of the saints, or the role of angels in God's plan.

This is a natural progression, as the Rosary is a gateway to a richer spiritual life. It connects you to the broader tapestry of faith, inspiring you to explore and deepen your understanding of God's love and presence.

5. Why Does the Rosary Sometimes Bring Sins to the Surface?

As you pray the Rosary, you may notice certain sins, struggles, or even a sense of spiritual attack rising to the surface. While this can feel overwhelming, it is actually a sign that your prayer is powerful and transformative. The Rosary is a prayer of purification, shifting your energetic frequency and awareness, which can disturb lower-level entities or reveal where darkness is hiding in your life.

Do not be discouraged. This is an opportunity for healing and growth in holiness. Continue praying the Rosary with trust, asking Mary for her guidance and strength. If you feel any demonic activity or disturbances, reach out to a trusted spiritual leader and consider praying in groups, such as a confraternity or with church members before Mass.

Many churches offer group Rosary sessions—check your local parish to join one. Know that God is leading you toward greater freedom, peace, and spiritual victory. However, always seek guidance from a medical professional in addition to consulting a trusted spiritual or religious leader..

6. Can Praying the Rosary Elevate My Spirituality?

Yes, a daily practice of praying the Rosary can elevate your spirituality in profound ways. Over time, you may find yourself experiencing:

- A deeper sense of God's presence in your life.
- Greater sensitivity to the Holy Spirit's guidance.
- Spiritual gifts such as prophetic dreams, discernment, or a heightened awareness of God's will.

These experiences are not the goal of praying the Rosary but rather a natural outgrowth of a life rooted in prayer and devotion. If you notice these changes, embrace them with humility and gratitude, and continue to seek Holy guidance in using these gifts for good.

7. Can I Choose a Rosary with Crystals That Align with My Intentions?

Yes, many people choose rosaries made with specific crystals that align with their intentions or petitions. The material of the beads can add a personal and symbolic touch to your prayer practice. Here are some popular crystals and their associated intentions:

- **Rose Quartz**: For self-love, healing, and emotional balance.
- **Amethyst**: For spiritual protection, clarity, and peace.
- **Jade**: For financial blessings, prosperity, and good fortune.
- **Citrine**: For abundance, creativity, and confidence.
- **Onyx**: For strength, grounding, and protection.
- **Lapis Lazuli**: For wisdom, truth, and spiritual insight.

When choosing a rosary, consider what resonates with your heart and intentions. Remember, the power of the Rosary lies in the prayers, not the materials, but the beads can serve as a meaningful reminder of your petitions.

8. What Are the Different Types of Rosaries?

There are many variations of the Rosary, each with its own focus and structure. Here are a few examples:

- **Traditional Rosary**: The most common form, with five decades and the Joyful, Sorrowful, Glorious, and Luminous Mysteries.
- **Seven Sorrows Rosary**: Focuses on the seven sorrows of Mary, with seven sets of seven beads.
- **Franciscan Crown Rosary**: Also known as the Seven Joys Rosary, it celebrates the joyful events in Mary's life.
- **Chaplet of Divine Mercy**: A shorter prayer that focuses on God's mercy, often prayed on a traditional Rosary.
- **Single-Decade Rosary**: A compact version with one decade, ideal for travel or quick prayers.
- **Chaplet of St. Michael**: A devotion to St. Michael the Archangel, consisting of nine salutations honoring the choirs of angels.
- **Chaplet of St. Anne**: A devotion to St. Anne, consisting of 3 Our Father Beads and 3 sets of 5 Hail Mary Beads
- **Chaplet of Our Lady of Silence:** A devotion to Our Lady of Silence consisting of 12 Our Father beads representing the 12 Virtues, 12 Hail Mary beads and 50 beads for the Jesus and Mary save Souls Prayer to be recited

Each type of Rosary offers a unique way to connect with Mary and deepen your prayer life. Choose the one that speaks to your heart and fits your spiritual needs.

9. Am I Connecting to Pagan Deities by Praying the Rosary?

It's natural to notice parallels between Mary and figures from other belief systems, such as Yemaya in African spirituality, Mokosh in Slavic mythology, Isis from ancient Egypt, or the Aztec goddess Tonantzin, often linked to Our Lady of Guadalupe. These commonalities stem from universal themes of nurturing, protection, and motherhood that transcend cultures and religions. Within the Catholic faith, however, the Rosary is a direct connection to Mary's divine energy and her intercession with God.

Interestingly, Christianity itself contains symbols and practices that can be traced back to earlier religions. The fish symbol, for example, was used in ancient pagan traditions as a sign of fertility and life before being adopted as a Christian symbol of faith. Similarly, the practice of baptism has roots in earlier purification rituals found in Judaism and even more ancient religions, symbolizing renewal and spiritual cleansing.

Mary, too, carries echoes of these connections. The Memorare, a well-known Catholic prayer invoking Mary's intercession, has been rumored to trace its origins back to prayers dedicated to the Egyptian goddess Isis. Likewise, images of Mary cradling the Christ Child bear a striking resemblance to depictions of Isis holding her son, Horus. These artistic and spiritual parallels highlight the ways in which universal archetypes of the divine feminine and motherhood have resonated across cultures and beliefs.

The beauty of prayer to Mary, however, lies in its deeply personal nature. When praying the Rosary, the aspect of Mary you connect with depends entirely on your intention. You may feel drawn to Our Lady of Guadalupe, honoring her as a symbol of compassion and cultural identity. Or, you might turn to Our Lady of Perpetual Help for guidance in times of trouble, or Our Lady of Czestochowa, revered for resilience and strength. Mary is multifaceted, as reflected in her many titles and roles celebrated in the Litany of Mary—Queen of Angels, Holy Mother of God, Comforter of the Afflicted, and more.

For some, prayer to Mary may also carry layers of cultural syncretism. For example, in Cuba, Our Lady of Charity (Virgen de la Caridad del Cobre) is often intertwined with the Yoruban goddess Ochún, while in Brazil, Our Lady of Aparecida is linked to Oxum. These connections originated from the history of enslaved peoples masking their traditional deities within Catholic imagery to preserve their spiritual practices.

Ultimately, praying the Rosary allows you to choose the connection that feels most meaningful to you. Whether you seek Mary as a compassionate mother, a symbol of cultural identity, or an intercessor with God, your prayers are directed toward the same Queen of Angels, the Holy Mother of God. Mary's many names, roles, and even her echoes in ancient traditions reflect her vast, loving presence, making her accessible to all who seek her grace.

10. Is "To Christ Through Mary" True?

The phrase "To Christ Through Mary" holds deep meaning for many, but it's important to clarify that having a devotion to Mary does not necessarily mean you are, or will become, a modern day Christian. For some, this connection to Mary leads to a transformative, mystical experience where they embody Christ consciousness—a state of compassion, love, and spiritual awakening. However, Mary does not demand conversion to the Catholic faith in order to have a relationship with her.

Throughout history, people of various spiritual paths have formed meaningful connections with Mary. Catholic witches, Pagans, Hoodoo practitioners, Muslims, and others have embraced Mary as a guiding presence without feeling called to abandon their own faiths. For many, this relationship enriches and strengthens their unique spiritual journey rather than completely altering it. Mary's universal love transcends religious boundaries, allowing people to connect with her on their own terms.

Ultimately, Mary's role as a nurturing, protective presence speaks to universal themes of divine love and grace. While "To Christ Through Mary" resonates deeply for some within a mystical or Christian framework, Mary's love is inclusive and accessible to anyone who seeks her, regardless of their faith or spiritual background.

11. Is Virgin Mary a Goddess?

For some, the Virgin Mary is revered as a Goddess. Various spiritual traditions and esoteric beliefs view her as a manifestation of divine feminine energy, associating her with figures like Sophia (wisdom personified) or even as a daughter of Isis, the ancient Egyptian Goddess. She is sometimes called the "Goddess of the West," embodying themes of compassion, nurturing, and divine protection.

However, in the modern Christian lens, Mary is not considered a Goddess. While Christian devotees often demonstrate deep reverence for her—kissing her statues, praying to her, and seeking her intercession—these acts are seen as honoring her unique role as the mother of Jesus, not ascribing divinity to her. Mary is venerated as a holy figure, a spiritual guide, and an intercessor, but not as a deity in Christian theology.

Ultimately, whether Mary is seen as a Goddess or not depends on the lens through which she is viewed. Her universal appeal as a symbol of love and grace continues to inspire devotion across diverse spiritual and religious perspectives.

12. Is Praying the Rosary Biblical?

Yes, praying the Rosary is deeply rooted in Scripture. The prayers within the Rosary are drawn directly from the Bible. For example, the "Hail Mary" prayer is based on the angel Gabriel's greeting to Mary in Luke 1:28, "Hail, full of grace, the Lord is with you," and Elizabeth's words in Luke 1:42, "Blessed are you among women, and blessed is the fruit of your womb."

The "Our Father," also known as the Lord's Prayer, comes directly from Jesus' teaching in Matthew 6:9-13, where He instructs His disciples on how to pray. Additionally, the Rosary's meditations focus on key events in the life of Jesus and Mary, encouraging reflection on the Gospel.

While the Rosary is not explicitly outlined in the Bible as a practice, its prayers and themes are undeniably scriptural, making it a powerful and biblical form of prayer for many Christians.

13. Is the Rosary a Punishment or Penance?

The Rosary is not a punishment but a beautiful gift. While it's true that priests may assign it as part of penance after confession, this is not meant to feel like a chore. Instead, it's because of the Rosary's incredible ability to bring cleansing, peace, and transformation. The Rosary allows for deep reflection, helps us grow closer to God, and fosters clarity and comfort in our spiritual lives.

Rather than seeing it as an obligation tied to guilt or shame, the Rosary should be embraced as an opportunity for healing and grace. Its repetition and meditative nature create a space for peace and renewal, making it a powerful spiritual tool. While it may take effort at times, it is not meant to feel like an unwilling chore but a pathway to deeper connection with God and a source of profound transformation.

14. Will I Still Achieve the Same Results if I am Unable to pray the Rosary while Meditating on the Mysteries?

Internal prayer while praying the Rosary does allow you to achieve a unique experience but there is no proof confirming that you will achieve more graces, etc. than if you pray the Rosary without it. If meditation feels challenging, don't let it stop you from praying altogether—you can still find peace and spiritual benefits by reciting the prayers with intention and sincerity. Some people find it helpful to look at sacred art for inspiration or simply reflect on the mystery when it's announced. The most important thing is your heartfelt intention and devotion, not the exact method you use. Focus on what feels meaningful and accessible to you, and trust that your efforts are enough.

15. Do I Need Physical Beads to Pray the Rosary?

No, you do not need physical beads to pray the Rosary. While beads are a helpful tool to count the prayers and keep track of the decades, they are not a requirement. You can use your fingers, your breath, or even follow along mentally to complete the prayers. The Rosary is, at its core, a means of meditative prayer and devotion, and the focus should always be on connecting with the Mysteries and fostering a heartfelt dialogue. Physical beads are simply a tool to assist in maintaining focus and rhythm during prayer, but they are not essential for the practice.

16. What if I Don't Believe Everything in the Creed?

It is absolutely fine if you do not fully align with every aspect of the Creed. The Rosary is a personal and customizable form of prayer, and what matters most is that it speaks to your heart and spirituality. You can choose to completely skip the Creed if it doesn't resonate with you or modify it in a way that feels authentic to your beliefs. For example, some people replace "Father" with "Mother" in their prayers or adjust other phrases to reflect their personal understanding of the Divine. Additionally, there are some rosaries that replace the traditional cross with a Marian pendant, which may feel more aligned with your spiritual journey. The Rosary is a tool for connection and reflection, and it should evolve to suit your spiritual needs.

17. Can I Use it as a Part of my Witchcraft or Magical Practice?

Yes, the Rosary can be incorporated into your witchcraft or magical practice, but it's important to approach it with respect and understanding. Tools, like the Rosary, are inherently neutral—they are neither good nor bad. Much like how a fork can be used to nourish oneself by eating or to harm someone by stabbing, the Rosary is a tool that reflects the intention and energy of the one using it. However, I've observed that those who lack a genuine devotion to Mother Mary—whether you call her Mary, Our Lady of Guadalupe, the Black Madonna, or another name—often see little to no success when picking up the Rosary for a selfish or one-time use.

Most spiritual workings require a relationship and reciprocal energy. If someone petitions a deity, saint, or energy without offering respect, devotion, or building a connection, they are likely to find their efforts ineffective. Mother Mary, in particular, is an energy connected to inner healing, the granting of graces, protection from demonic influence, and miracles. These miracles may include financial blessings, but she is not typically associated with granting petitions related to control or manipulation, such as bringing an ex-lover back or enforcing one's will over another. Her energy is aligned with maturation of the soul and guiding individuals toward spiritual growth, not exerting control over others—even if the intent seems altruistic.

I was deeply disturbed when I came across a video of a woman attempting to use the Rosary in a manipulative manner. She was trying to control her husband and manifest a very specific amount of money. Watching her misuse something sacred in such a selfish and disrespectful way felt jarring, and her actions were a clear desecration of the sanctity of the Rosary. Such approaches typically do not succeed in the name of Mother Mary, as her energy is rooted in healing, compassion, and grace—not control or exploitation. Approaching the Rosary with an open heart and genuine reverence is key to experiencing its true spiritual power.

18. Is it Okay to use a Rosary that Belonged to Someone Else?

Yes, it is absolutely okay to use a rosary that belonged to someone else. It's important to remember that rosaries are often mass-produced by individuals who may not be believers and who might not always be in the best of moods during the production and distribution process. This means that the beads themselves have already been touched and handled by several people before reaching you. However, by praying your prayers on the rosary, you will naturally infuse it with your own energy, making it a personal and sacred tool for your spiritual practice. That being said, if you feel a dark or unsettling energy coming from the rosary itself, trust your intuition. It is perfectly fine—and not at all silly or wrong—to choose not to use it in such a case. Respect your feelings and seek a rosary that feels aligned with your spiritual intentions.

The Rosary is a gift that continues to reveal its beauty and power the more you pray it. Whether you are seeking healing, guidance, or a deeper connection to God, the Rosary is a faithful companion on your spiritual journey. Embrace it with an open heart, and let Mary lead you closer to her Son.

19. Is it Better to Pray in Latin?

Praying in Latin holds a special place in Catholic tradition and spirituality. Latin, as the sacred language of the Church, is often described as having unique spiritual power. Some believe that demons dislike Latin, which is why it is frequently used in exorcisms. The unchangeable nature of Latin has preserved its meaning and force across centuries, providing consistency and clarity in prayer. This makes it a language of unity, connecting those across the world who join in prayer, regardless of nationality or culture.

Furthermore, praying in Latin ties us to the prayers of our ancestors, invoking a sense of continuity and shared faith. Latin's deep history in the Church imbues it with a sense of reverence and energy, making it a powerful tool for spiritual practices. Many feel that the act of praying in Latin helps them engage more profoundly with the divine and connect to the universal Church.

That said, it is important to remember that the heart of prayer lies in personal intention and faith. Whether you choose to pray in Latin or your mother tongue, the sincerity and openness of your heart are what truly matter. The Rosary, whether recited in Latin, English, or any other language, remains a beautiful and effective devotion. Pray in the language that uplifts your spirit and draws you closer to God. There is no "better" or "worse" when it comes to truly heartfelt prayer.

20. Why Does Mary Ask Us to Pray the Rosary?

Mary's repeated call for us to pray the Rosary, especially during her apparitions in times of great trial or impending genocide can be believed to prevent catastrophic events and bring forth reconciliation.

Another answer is that Mary enjoys our prayers and magnifies them. Her soul is known as the "Magnificat" because she exalts and reflects

God's glory through her pure love and humility. Mystics believe that when we pray to her, it delights her as a loving mother and gracious queen. Mary does not seek our prayers out of vanity but because sincere, heartfelt prayer opens our hearts to God's grace. Praying the Rosary, in particular, weaves a spiritual protection for our souls, like a garland of heavenly roses offered to her. As an attributed mystical revelation states, "When you pray the Rosary, it is as if you are handing me roses, and I weave them into a garland of protection for your soul." This image of a crown of light, created from our prayers, reminds us of the power of devotion and the maternal care Mary provides for each of her children.

21. Is the Rosary for Young People?

Absolutely, the Rosary is for people of all ages, including young people. While some of the mysteries, such as the Scourging at the Pillar or the Crucifixion, might be more intense and require thoughtful explanation for younger participants, the overall prayer is accessible to everyone. The Rosary offers a structure that allows individuals to grow in their faith and deepen their relationship with God, no matter their stage in life. For young people, simpler reflections on the mysteries that highlight God's love, grace, and care can make the Rosary meaningful and age-appropriate. By introducing the Rosary early, it provides a foundation for spiritual growth, instilling a rhythm of prayer and devotion that can guide them throughout their lives.

22. Can I Pray the Rosary on a Santa Muerte Rosary or a Witch's Rosary?

Yes, you can pray the Rosary on a Santa Muerte Rosary or a Witch's Rosary, but it's important to note that their structure may differ from a traditional Rosary. For example, a Santa Muerte Rosary typically follows the traditional 59-bead structure, though its design and symbols may vary. A Witch's Rosary, however, might not follow the sets of ten beads for the Hail Mary prayers, requiring you to adapt your prayers accordingly.

That said, it's generally preferred to pray on a Rosary created specifically for Marian energy, as it aligns with traditional devotion to the Virgin Mary. However, if your practices are syncretic, or if you see the Virgin Mary as a goddess coexisting with others in your spiritual path, it's okay to use a Rosary dedicated to another entity if it feels right to you. The key is your intention and focus during prayer. If using a non-traditional Rosary makes you feel uneasy or conflicted, it may be better to stick to one aligned with Marian devotion. Ultimately, your spiritual connection and comfort are what matter most.

23: Do I Have to Pray the Rosary all at Once?

No, you do not need to pray all five decades of the Rosary at one time. It is perfectly fine to pray the Rosary throughout the day, breaking it into smaller sessions as your schedule allows. What matters most is the sincerity and focus you bring to your prayers, not the timing or length of each session. Feel free to pause and return to the Rosary whenever it fits into your day, as long as your heart remains centered on prayer and reflection.

24: Is it Okay for Me to Wear my Rosary?

Yes, it is okay to wear your Rosary. There is no official rule declaring that you cannot wear it, so feel free to do so. Many people even choose to purchase Rosaries with stretchy elastic designed to be worn as bracelets—these are especially convenient for those who like to pray on the go. Wearing a Rosary can also hold personal significance for many individuals. Some view it as a talisman, feeling a sense of protection and confidence because of the powerful prayers associated with it. However, it is important to approach this practice with respect, using the Rosary as a tool for prayer and reflection rather than merely as a fashion accessory.

25. Can I Manifest with the Rosary?

Yes, the Rosary is often used by people to pray for a change in their own lives and in the lives of others. Many mystics, as well as practitioners of Hoodoo and Catholic folk witches, recognize the Rosary and its mysteries as powerful tools for manifestation. These groups often view the mysteries within the Rosary as keys and codes for bringing desires into reality. They see them as profound teachings that guide how to manifest effectively. For instance, the Joyful Mysteries illustrate the process of creation—receiving an idea, saying yes to it, nurturing it, and patiently waiting for its fruition.

There is nothing wrong with using the Rosary as a tool for manifestation, provided it's approached with reverence and respect rather than as a simple transaction. When used sincerely and prayerfully, the Rosary can align one's intentions with divine will, allowing manifestations to unfold naturally and in harmony with a higher plan. This long-standing practice shows how spiritual traditions can be deeply intertwined with the art of manifesting.

26. Why do I Feel Bad During or after Praying the Rosary?

It is not uncommon to feel discomfort during or after praying the Rosary, and this experience can arise for various reasons. Sometimes, certain mysteries may not resonate at a particular time, and your body might be signaling the need to step back. Other times, the unease could stem from inner resistance, unresolved struggles, or even spiritual "blockages, your own "demons fighting to hold on. In these moments, discernment is key. Only you can determine if the discomfort is a sign to pause or an invitation to press forward in faith.

For many, resistance to the Rosary can also be tied to deeper issues, such as negative associations with the Church or even religious trauma. If your relationship with the Church has been fraught, it can be hard to separate Mary from the institution she is often so deeply intertwined with. For some, the act of praying the Rosary may bring up emotional wounds, feelings of alienation, or even anger tied to past experiences. This makes it even more challenging to connect with Mary on a personal or spiritual level, as she may feel indistinguishable from the Church and its negative connotations. Healing this relationship takes time, and it's important to approach it with patience and self-compassion. If you work with other deities or spiritual entities, you might feel their presence or even their claim on you when engaging with the Rosary. This can manifest as a sense of conflict or resistance, as these energies interact or express their wishes regarding your spiritual path. Acknowledge and respect these dynamics as they may hold important insights about your spiritual alignment and the practices that best support your journey. It's also worth remembering that the Rosary is not a requirement for connection with the divine. If the practice feels uncomfortable or incompatible with your spiritual path, there is no obligation to force it.

The Rosary is a sacred tool meant to draw you closer to Mary and deepen your spiritual practice, but if you cannot yet reconcile your feelings about the Church or religious trauma, it may not feel right. If you are highly sensitive you may feel the sacred technology working as well. For instance, some people might experience physical sensations, like tingling in their third eye while meditating on the mysteries, signaling that their energy centers are being activated or that another form of prayer might be better for them at this moment. Ultimately, whether or not the Rosary becomes part of your spiritual journey is a deeply personal decision. Pay attention to how your body and spirit feel and take appropriate action.

It's essential to listen to divine guidance rather than fear or unresolved resistance to find what truly resonates with you. Know that the Rosary is not the only means of connection to Mary nor is it the only way to pray and reflect on the mysteries.

Anielle Reid is a mystic and author who has written *The Hoodoo Rosary, The People's Rosary* and several oracle decks like *The Magick and Mediums Oracle, The Slavic Oracle, The Golden Light Oracle* and *The Latin Love Oracle.*

www.ingramcontent.com/pod-product-compliance
Lightning Source LLC
Chambersburg PA
CBHW071228070526
44583CB00017B/2095